Tortoises
Terrapins & Turtles
of Africa

Bill Branch

Struik Publishers
(a division of New Holland Publishing (South Africa) (Pty) Ltd)
Cornelis Struik House
80 McKenzie Street
Cape Town 8001

New Holland Publishing is a division of Avusa Ltd

Visit us at **www.struik.co.za**
Log on to our photographic website
www.imagesofafrica.co.za for an African experience.

First published in 2008

Publishing manager: Pippa Parker
Managing editor: Helen de Villiers
Editor: Leonie Hofmeyr-Juritz
Project co-ordinator: Gill Gordon
Design Director: Janice Evans
Designer: Louise Topping
Proofreader: Glynne Newlands
Cartographer: Neil Bester

Reproduction by Hirt & Carter Cape (Pty) Ltd
Printed and bound by CTP Book Printers

ISBN 978 1 77007 463 7

TITLE PAGE: Tortoise shells. ABOVE: Juvenile Leatherback Sea Turtle. OPPOSITE LEFT TO RIGHT: Tent Tortoise, Okavango Hinged
Terrapin, Loggerhead Sea Turtle. PAGE 6: Verroux's Tent Tortoise; PAGE 30: African Spurred Tortoise; PAGE 70: Marsh
Terrapin; PAGE 106: Loggerhead Sea Turtle.

Contents

Leopard Tortoise in the Swartkop River, Namibia.

Preface

Although southern Africa is a biodiversity hotspot and South Africa is home to the world's richest diversity of tortoises, there have been relatively few popular books that introduce the lives of these fascinating reptiles to the interested naturalist. Terrapins are much more diverse in tropical Africa, where they swim in the major rivers, rift lakes, marshes and swamps. Sea turtles glide gracefully throughout Africa's coastal waters, but continue to nest on only a few sheltered and protected beaches. Africa's reptile wealth deserves to be better known, and this small volume takes a step in that direction.

The coverage of this book is restricted to sub-Saharan Africa and its coastal islands. The relatively few species on the Indian Ocean islands have been excluded, as the taxonomy of some of these forms is unresolved, whilst others have been relatively recently introduced. Similarly, the small radiation of tortoises and terrapins along the coastal regions of North Africa has not been covered. There is much scientific debate about just how many species are found in these two regions. Moreover, those in North Africa represent a relatively recent radiation, and are more closely related to Eurasian species. Kemp's Ridley Sea Turtle is mainly restricted to the western Atlantic, with only a few vagrant specimens known from the Atlantic off North Africa. It is not known to breed on African beaches, or to undergo feeding migrations to African waters, and so is also excluded from this book.

With these limitations, the 46 species of chelonians found in sub-Saharan Africa are covered; together they represent nearly 15 per cent of the world's chelonians. This field guide describes how to identify these species, where they are likely to be found, and summarises their lives in simple terms to help the interested naturalist.

BILL BRANCH

Acknowledgements

All field guides build on previous observations and research accumulated by many people. This book compiles this body of knowledge; a small fraction of the related synthetic material is summarised in Resources (page 124). Only within the last 25 years have detailed studies on the ecology of the chelonians in Africa begun. Significant recent work in southern Africa has been undertaken at the University of the Western Cape by Reitha Hofmeyr and her students and colleagues, particularly Victor Loehr and Brian Heenan. Elsewhere in Africa, the studies of Luca

Leopard Tortoise.

Luselli, Adrian Hailey and Jonathan Kabigumila have increased our knowledge of the lives of other species. Dieter Gramentz has undertaken a series of studies of the ecology of African soft-shelled terrapins, Trionycidae, culminating in two definitive monographs. The detailed taxonomic studies of Roger Bour (Museum National d'Historie Naturelle, Paris) continue to reveal new species of African chelonians, with the discovery of two new species of Hinged terrapin in the last five years. Field work in Africa is often difficult and dangerous, but this does not deter colleagues such as Marius Burger, Luca Luselli, Jerome Maran, Thomas Mazuch, Olivier Pauwels or Colin Tilbury. Bernard Devaux and his colleagues at SOPTOM, France, have sparked public interest in chelonians worldwide, and have also been instrumental in protecting endangered tortoises in Senegal and Madagascar with their innovative 'Tortoise Villages'.

The species maps derive from numerous sources: my own, and those of the database of the *South African Reptile Atlas*, for southern African species; those for side-necked terrapins from the studies of Don Broadley and Roger Bour; and the general and regional maps of African chelonians for a variety of other species, by John Iverson, Bernard Devaux and Carl Ernst. I also thank George Hughes who read and gently corrected the section on sea turtles.

A number of colleagues assisted with photographs of rare or restricted species, or allowed me to replace my slides with their more artistic studies. For these I thank Graham Alexander, Roger Bour, Bernard Devaux, Jacques Fretey, Dieter Gramentz, George Hughes, Victor Loehr, Colin McRae, Johan Marais, Jerome Maran, Thomas Mazuch, Johan Measey, Olivier Pauwels, Mark-Oliver Roedel and Colin Tilbury. A special thanks to Marius Burger, whose tortoise photography is just too good; if he could only look after his camera lenses as well as his hair...

Finally, Pippa Parker, publisher for the Natural History section at Struik, continues to show faith in my abilities and, with her editorial and design teams, led by Helen de Villiers and Janice Evans respectively, produces stunning books that are a credit to any author; the phrase 'silk purses from pigs' ears' comes to mind! For this book, special thanks are due to the designer, Louise Topping, and editor, Leonie Hofmeyr-Juritz.

Introduction

What are tortoises, terrapins and turtles?

Common names are confusing, and what is called a 'turtle' in the Americas is called a 'terrapin' in South Africa, while in Australia it was once called a 'freshwater tortoise' and is now known as a 'freshwater turtle'. 'Tortoise', 'terrapin' and 'turtle' have no fixed meanings, and the names are best used simply to differentiate species that live on land, in fresh water and in the sea, respectively. The names describe where they live, and not necessarily how closely related they are to other species. The word 'tortoise' is derived from the old French word *tortis*, meaning 'twisted'; the name 'turtle' is probably a corruption of the same word. Tortoises were once common in southern Europe, and the French name may have been applied because of the curiously bent forelegs that all tortoises have. The origin of the name 'terrapin' remains obscure. Scientifically, they constitute an order of reptiles called the Chelonia, or Shield Reptiles. As a group, tortoises, terrapins and turtles are best called chelonians – their correct, if presently unfamiliar, common name.

Natal Hinged Tortoise.

Origins

Chelonians have been around for a long time. They are the oldest surviving reptile lineage, having plodded and swum their way through over 220 million years of earth's history. They arose before the dinosaurs, when the land was populated by the early reptiles familiar to many South Africans from the reconstructions of Karoo fossils; at this time the mammal-like reptiles first appeared, and some palaeontologists justifiably argue that chelonians are more closely related to mammals than to any other living reptile group. This does not suggest that they gave rise to mammals; rather, they are not very closely related to other surviving reptiles. During their history they have seen the rise and fall of the dinosaurs, survived Armageddon's asteroids, and have drifted to the corners of the globe on the wandering continents. Now they face their greatest challenge, the destruction of their habitats and the world's biodiversity by

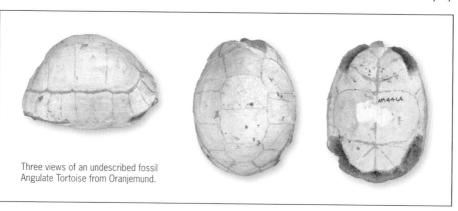

Three views of an undescribed fossil Angulate Tortoise from Oranjemund.

A Karoo Tent Tortoise walking on a rock bearing a Karoo fossil.

man – either directly, through exploitation, or through human indifference to the effects of global warming and habitat destruction.

The probable ancestry of chelonians is an ongoing debate, but it is contentious only because so few fossils survive from long ago. Those that have, are understandably scattered and fragmented. One candidate ancestor is a small, rat-sized vertebrate, called *Eunotosaurus africanus,* from South African Upper Permian rocks that are 260 million years old. It had enlarged, thickened ribs that could be seen as an intermediate stage in the evolution of the chelonian carapace, but had not yet lost its teeth, and its shoulder blades were outside its rib cage. There are other possible ancestral candidates (*Captorhinus, Bradysaurus* and *Anthodon*), but none possess the full suite of chelonian features, and resolution of the problem awaits further discoveries.

The identity of the first undisputed chelonian fossil also remains unresolved. For many years it was considered to be *Proganochelys quenstedti* from the Upper Triassic, 220 million years ago (Ma) in Germany. Already in this long-extinct chelonian, the characteristic arrangement of the shell plates, or scutes, was evident. Its neck, however, was still long and could not be withdrawn under the shell, and teeth were still present. Similar fossils, from the Early Triassic, have recently been discovered in South Africa, in the Elliot Formation at Clocolan in the Free State. More recently, another German candidate, from the Lower Ladinian, Middle Triassic (230 Ma), was discovered – *Priscochelys hegnabrunensis*. It is, however, difficult to be sure of its status, as it is known from a single shell fragment, only a

Fossil of a possible chelonian ancestor (*Eunotosaurus africanus*).

Modern pelomedusids, such as the Marsh Terrapin, evolved in Africa.

few centimetres in diameter. The problem with assigning such fragments is that no one really knows from which fossil group chelonians evolved. Moreover, it is not the only problematic fossil that has sometimes been seen as a chelonian.

Although there has been debate as to whether early chelonians evolved in aquatic habitats or on the land, recent evidence supports the latter claim. No early chelonians show aquatic adaptations, and none have been found in unequivocally aquatic habitats. What is known, however, is that soon after chelonians arose they quickly diversified and invaded aquatic habitats.

The two major groups of living chelonians arose at this time, with *Proganochelys* possibly giving rise to the Pleurodira (side-necked chelonians), whilst the Cryptodira (hidden-necked chelonians) arose soon afterwards. At this time, in the Middle Jurassic (180–154 Ma), dinosaurs, crocodiles, lizards and chelonians were all diversifying. Ancestors of modern soft-shelled terrapins, Trionychidae, arose in Asia. The earliest known sea turtles appear in the fossil record in the Late Jurassic period, about 144 Ma, although they belong to now extinct families. The most dramatic of these was *Archelon ischyros*, of the Protostegidae, which lived from 144 to 65 Ma, and had a shell 3 metres long and paddle-like flippers spanning 5 metres.

With the increasing diversification of aquatic chelonians in the Upper Cretaceous (99–66 Ma), both the characteristic side-necked terrapins of Africa, the Pelomedusidae and modern sea turtles, Cheloniidae, arose. A massive meteorite impact is thought to have brought to an end the Cretaceous, with the extinction of the giant dinosaurs and many fossil chelonians. With the loss of the dinosaurs, the Age of Reptiles gave way to the Age of Mammals, although four families of marine turtles survived. Two, the Cheloniidae and Dermochelyidae, still swim the oceans, but the Toxochelyidae became extinct during the Eocene, and Protostegidae during the Oligocene.

The oldest known tortoises, Testudinidae, date from the late Paleocene (58–56 Ma in Mongolia, and by the early Eocene, they had plodded their way to Europe and North America, but never got to the isolated, drifting continent of Australia. They first appeared in Africa in the Late Eocene (about 35.5 Ma), based on a giant species, *Gigantochersina ammon* collected in Egypt.

In the Miocene (about 20 Ma), the modern African chelonian genera began to appear, with the ancestors of *Geochelone sulcata* arriving from Asia; at the same time, modern terrapins including the soft-shelled *Cyclanorbis* as well as the modern pelomedusids, *Pelomedusa* and *Pelusios,* evolved in Africa. By 5 Ma, the modern chelonian fauna of sub-Saharan Africa has essentially been established.

Diversity and classification

Living chelonians form only a fragment of their fossil diversity, and four suborders, containing 25 families, are recognised; half of these are now extinct. Modern forms fall into two major groups: the Pleurodira (side-necked chelonians) and the Cryptodira (hidden-necked chelonians). The groups differ most obviously in the way in which the head is withdrawn, and with the secondary loss, in the Cryptodira, of fusion of the pelvis with the carapace.

There are additional differences between the groups (see box below). Globally, chelonians are now represented by two families of side-necked chelonians and 11 families of hidden-necked chelonians. Indigenous chelonians of sub-Saharan Africa include members from a single terrestrial family, Testudinidae, two freshwater terrapin families, Pelomedusidae and Trionycidae, and two families of sea turtle, Cheloniidae and Dermochelyidae. A single terrapin species from another family, Emydidae, is occasionally introduced.

Characteristics of two major groups of living chelonians

Feature	Cryptodira	Pleurodira
Head and neck	Head withdrawn by vertical flexure. Protected by forelimbs. Neck skin can invaginate.	Head withdrawn sideways. Not protected by forelimbs. Neck skin cannot invaginate.
Plastron scutes	Six pairs; only anterior gulars may fuse. Horny scutes lost in some groups (soft-shells).	Six pairs, plus an anterior intergular. Horny scutes never lost.
Pelvic girdle	Pelvis not fused to shell; attached by ligaments.	Pelvis fused to shell.
Skull structure	Skull reinforced with pterygoid bone.	Skull reinforced with quadrate bone.

People are most likely to see chelonians in their natural habitat and so the following discussion does not follow strict classification. Freshwater chelonians (terrapins) fall into two different suborders and three different families, but are discussed together.

Verroux's Tent Tortoise.

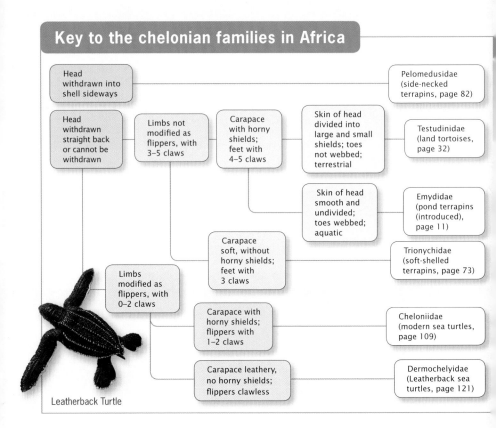

Key to the chelonian families in Africa

- Head withdrawn into shell sideways → Pelomedusidae (side-necked terrapins, page 82)
- Head withdrawn straight back or cannot be withdrawn
  - Limbs not modified as flippers, with 3–5 claws
    - Carapace with horny shields; feet with 4–5 claws
      - Skin of head divided into large and small shields; toes not webbed; terrestrial → Testudinidae (land tortoises, page 32)
      - Skin of head smooth and undivided; toes webbed; aquatic → Emydidae (pond terrapins (introduced), page 11)
    - Carapace soft, without horny shields; feet with 3 claws → Trionychidae (soft-shelled terrapins, page 73)
  - Limbs modified as flippers, with 0–2 claws
    - Carapace with horny shields; flippers with 1–2 claws → Cheloniidae (modern sea turtles, page 109)
    - Carapace leathery, no horny shields; flippers clawless → Dermochelyidae (Leatherback sea turtles, page 121)

Leatherback Turtle

Anatomy

Crocodiles, the tuatara, snakes and lizards, and chelonians, as well as the dinosaurs, pterodactyls, plesiosaurs, and numerous other extinct groups, are all reptiles. These diverse groups give us very little insight into the characteristic features of the class Reptilia. It is ill defined and used as a catch-all to hold diverse terrestrial vertebrates that develop without the tadpole stage of amphibians, the fur, milk and warm blood of mammals, or the feathers and warm blood of birds.

A primitive feature of the skull of chelonians, and all reptiles, is the single occipital condyle – the knob on the back of the skull that articulates with the backbone. The group is further characterised by having only a single bone in each ear, and with each half of the lower jaw being composed of several bones. Primitive reptiles and chelonians have a solid skull, with no large openings in its sides (an anapsid skull), although there is now some controversy as to whether this is secondarily derived in chelonians. Fertilisation is internal, and males have a single penis as do crocodiles, unlike the paired hemipenes of snakes and lizards.

Although some early tortoises had teeth, these are absent in all living species. Instead they have a horny beak, similar in appearance and function to that of a parrot. It may have a number of additional cusps or a serrated edge, and the sharp edges can cut soft tissues effectively, but the beak has no grinding surfaces, and so chelonians cannot chew their food.

Head of a Natal Hinged Tortoise.

Armour

The chelonian shell is unique among vertebrates, and its armour is rivalled only by the plated protection of the armadillo, or the bony dome of a box fish. It is divided into an upper carapace, a lower plastron and a connecting bridge along the sides. The shell may be soft, leathery, hard, flat, knobbed or hinged, but it is unlike anything else in the reptile world. It is a complex structure, composed of an outer horny layer that covers a regular mosaic of connected bones (rather like those of the human skull), which are fused to the rib cage. This entails some radical rearrangements in tortoise anatomy, not the least of which is the placing of both the pectoral and the pelvic girdles within the rib cage.

Shell components

The horny outer layer of the shell is composed of keratin (the same material that forms the basis of hair, finger nails and rhino horn), and is arranged in juxtaposed pieces, called scutes. These form a typical pattern on the carapace and plastron (see illustration on page 14), albeit with minor differences between species and individuals.

The underlying bones also have a regular, though more complex arrangement. To maintain the structural strength of the shell, the joins between the scutes and the bone sutures do not overlap.

In all tortoises, large windows are present in both the carapace and the plastron during development of the shell. These are rather like the fontanelle in the skull of a human baby. These gaps usually close with age, but persist in adults of some species, such as the Pancake Tortoise and Nama Padloper. During growth, new bone is added at the edges of the individual bones, which form wavy sutures as they come into contact. Growth ceases only in very old individuals, in which the bony shell becomes completely ossified.

The horny scutes of most tortoises show distinctive rings. The scutes grow by deposition of new material over the entire base, and this causes the scutes to grow pyramid-like. In many seasonally cold or dry climates, growth is intermittent, and greater in some parts of the year than others. The periods of reduced growth appear on the surface of the scute-like grooves, resembling tree rings, between the periods of greater growth. These rings may be laid down once a year, and thus allow a rough estimate of the age of the tortoise. However, in some regions with two wet seasons, growth rings may be laid down twice a year, thus confusing age determination. Moreover, as the scutes rise up, they become worn away at the apex, and the younger layers are lost. Most old tortoises develop smooth shells that are worn with age.

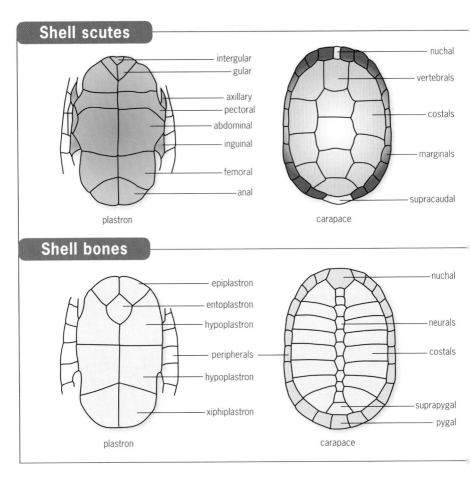

Shell scutes

plastron
- intergular
- gular
- axillary
- pectoral
- abdominal
- inguinal
- femoral
- anal

carapace
- nuchal
- vertebrals
- costals
- marginals
- supracaudal

Shell bones

plastron
- epiplastron
- entoplastron
- hypoplastron
- peripherals
- hypoplastron
- xiphiplastron

carapace
- nuchal
- neurals
- costals
- suprapygal
- pygal

Weight constraints

Although the shell forms a protective amour, its weight limits locomotion: chelonians are not famed for their speed. It takes a lot of energy for aquatic species to move this heavy shell through water, as they must frequently return to the surface to breathe and feed. Many terrapins have therefore evolved lighter shells, due to the loss of much of the underlying bone. In soft-shelled terrapins, not only is the bone of the shell greatly reduced; the horny layer, too, has lost much of its bulk. Although this weight reduction makes it easier for terrapins to swim, it does mean that much of

their protective armour is also lost. To avoi predators, many soft-shelled terrapins fora only at night, and also conceal themselves l shuffling down into the soft lake bed. Mar side-necked terrapins live only in tempora ponds or marshes, where predators such crocodiles and large fish are absent.

Hinges

In some species the bone sutures becom invaded with soft tissue to allow for a flexib hinge. This occurs in different regions shell, depending upon the group. In Hing terrapins, *Pelusios*, the hinge runs across t plastron between the humeral and pectoral scutes. It closes the front of the shell, protecting the head and forelimbs. In Hinged tortoises, *Kinixys*, the hinge is less flexible; it is situated at the back of the bridge, usually between marginals 7 and 8, and runs on to the rear of the carapace between costals 3 and 4. When closed, it makes access to the hind limbs and tail very difficult.

This hinge may initially have evolved to ease egg-laying in females. In very small tortoises, such as the Speckled Padloper, where the diameter of the relatively large egg is greater than the normal rear opening of the shell, soft seams in the rear of the female shell are essential for egg-laying. Just prior to egg-laying these rear sutures soften to allow for the passage of the egg, and then harden again. No permanent hinge is formed.

Domes

The high domed shell of the Leopard Tortoise increases the body cavity for the large lungs and developing eggs. The lungs lie above the guts, forming an air cavity above the vital organs. This provides extra protection from the sun's heat, allowing the Leopard Tortoise to withstand high body temperatures, and thus enter more open habitats and feed for longer periods than is possible for smaller species. Tenting of shell scutes also structurally reinforces and strengthens the shell; and the increased shell diameter challenges potential predators, which require a greater gape to seize the tortoise.

large Leopard Tortoise plods along a Karoo track.

Where chelonians live

Chelonians occur in aquatic, oceanic and terrestrial environments across tropical and temperate zones. They are widespread in sub-Saharan Africa, except for desert dunes and alpine grassland.

Terrestrial habitats

Tortoises are the only chelonians in Africa that live permanently on land and most species never willingly enter water. An exception is the Leopard Tortoise, which shows a surprising fondness for water and can regularly be found floating in small vleis and lakes. Female terrapins must come ashore to lay their eggs, and some species shelter underground when the seasonal wetlands they inhabit dry up. Otherwise, terrapins come on land only to bask.

Tortoise distributions are mainly linked to the major vegetation types, with many species restricted to one habitat type, e.g. grassland or desert (see table below). Others are more flexible in their habitat associations. The Leopard Tortoise lives in woodlands, scrublands and forests from South Africa to Ethiopia. Hinged tortoises form two main radiations: two species live in forests and four species inhabit savannah woodlands. Each of the five species of small Padlopers inhabits a different vegetation type, ranging from rocky desert to montane grassland.

Distribution of tortoise species

SPECIES	D	SD	SAW	MW	LF	MFG	FM
African Spurred Tortoise		●	●				
Angulate Tortoise		●					●
Parrot-beaked Tortoise							●
Karoo Padloper		●	●				
Boulenger's Padloper		●					
Speckled Padloper		●					
Nama Padloper	●						
Bell's Hinged Tortoise			●	●			
Forest Hinged Tortoise					●		
Home's Hinged Tortoise					●		
Lobatse Hinged Tortoise			●				
Natal Hinged Tortoise				●			
Speke's Hinged Tortoise			●	●			
Pancake Tortoise			●	●			
Geometric Tortoise							●
Serrated Tortoise		●	●				
Tent tortoises	●	●	●				
Leopard Tortoise		●	●	●	●	●	

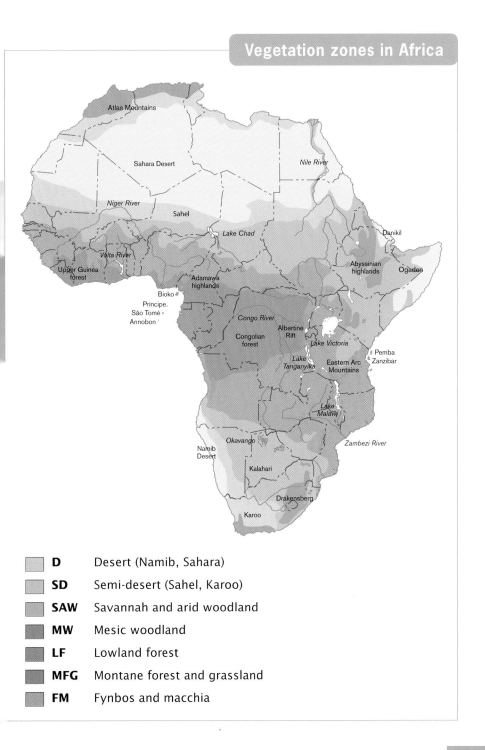

Vegetation zones in Africa

Atlas Mountains
Sahara Desert
Nile River
Niger River
Sahel
Lake Chad
Danikil
Volta River
Upper Guinea forest
Adamawa highlands
Abyssinian highlands
Ogaden
Bioko
Príncipe
São Tomé
Annobon
Congo River
Albertine Rift
Congolian forest
Lake Victoria
Pemba
Zanzibar
Lake Tanganyika
Eastern Arc Mountains
Lake Malawi
Okavango
Zambezi River
Namib Desert
Kalahari
Drakensberg
Karoo

D	Desert (Namib, Sahara)
SD	Semi-desert (Sahel, Karoo)
SAW	Savannah and arid woodland
MW	Mesic woodland
LF	Lowland forest
MFG	Montane forest and grassland
FM	Fynbos and macchia

Freshwater habitats

Terrapins live in various types of aquatic habitat, depending on their biology. Much of Africa is dry, with irregular rainfall; many African wetlands are therefore temporary and seasonal. As an adaptation to these cyclic droughts, some hinged terrapins dig underground in dry periods and lie dormant – a practice known as 'aestivating' – until the rains return. When the swamps flood again and the freshwater wetlands fill up, terrapins arise from their temporary tombs to resume their lives. Soft-shelled terrapins do not do this, and thus live only in association with permanent water, such as the major rivers or lakes. Nile soft-shelled terrapins can withstand brackish water, and often live in lagoons and estuaries. They can even survive short periods in the sea when washed out into the ocean during heavy floods. This has allowed them to colonise the lower reaches of many rivers, particularly along the Atlantic seaboard.

Marine habitats

Only sea turtles live permanently in the oceans. The species all show subtle differences in their diets, which are reflected in the habitats in which they forage. The Leatherback is the only pelagic turtle that feeds in the open ocean, both at the surface and at extreme depth (to 1 200 m). The Green Sea Turtle is the most vegetarian of the turtles, and often enters estuaries and shallow lagoons to feed on sea grasses. The other species show varying degrees of carnivory and food specialisation. The Hawksbill Turtle inhabits coral reefs, where it searches for sponges and sea urchins. The Olive Ridley Turtle feeds on crabs and shrimps, and can forage in shallow sandy seas and mangrove swamps. The large Loggerhead Turtle hunts conches and other hard shellfish around coral reefs and rocky areas.

A large Loggerhead Turtle swims across Aliwal Reef, South Africa.

Biology

Feeding

Tortoises are noted plodders, and feed mainly on sedentary or slow-moving food. They are almost exclusively herbivorous, although Hinged tortoises will also eat millipedes and animal faeces. Terrapins are generally omnivorous, feeding mainly on invertebrates. Some capture prey such as fish and frogs, usually by concealment and ambush. The lighter shell of the Marsh Terrapin allows it to ambush frogs, and even play 'crocodile', catching small birds that come to drink at the water's edge. Many terrapins capture prey using the suction caused by the rapid gaping of the mouth, combined with the depression of the throat floor by the hyoid bones. This creates a vacuum in the mouth, into which the water rushes, carrying the prey. Once caught, the victim has to be manipulated so that it can be swallowed; it is usually softened by many crunching movements of the jaws. Sea turtles specialise in foods such as sponges, molluscs and shrimps. It seems perverse that the Leatherback, the world's largest sea turtle, survives almost solely on a diet of watery jellyfish.

Are tortoises more important than antelope for seed dispersal?

In many areas, tortoises are found in high densities, and their biomass, measured as the weight of tortoises per hectare, can exceed that of many antelope species. In mesic thicket habitat in Addo Elephant National Park, in South Africa's Eastern Cape province, the Leopard and Angulate tortoise biomass is 12 to 13 per cent that of all mammalian herbivores. This means that the total weight of tortoises in the park is almost equal to the combined weight of kudu, buffalo, eland and bushbuck, and is exceeded in the area only by that of elephants. Tortoises are inefficient feeders, as they do not chew their food, and they also lack the specialised gut vats and bacteria that aid cows and antelope to digest cellulose. This means that tortoises have to eat large quantities of plants and, as a result, their faeces, or scats, are full of undamaged seeds. Like elephants, tortoises are important dispersers of seeds, especially as they often defecate inside bushes, where seeds that are passed have a better chance of germination than those scattered by elephants in the open.

Western Hinged Tortoise spreading seeds.

Angulate Tortoise drinking in the rain.

Dependence on water

Many tortoises live in arid or semi-arid areas where water is rare. Even savannah species are often faced with dry seasons when water bodies dry up and standing water is unavailable. Tortoises have a number of tricks that allow them to withstand these dry spells. Their skin is dry and impermeable, so that water loss through the skin is greatly reduced. In addition, tortoises avoid activity during the heat of the day, not just to escape overheating, but also to avoid water loss from dry wind.

Tortoises that live on sandy soils often have no access to standing water. To harvest the rain water when it falls, they have evolved a novel drinking behaviour. The tortoise extends its back legs fully, raising the height of the rear body. It fully extends its front legs and neck forward, and pushes the front edge of its carapace down hard against them, thereby tilting its shell forward and twisting the lower parts of the forelimbs so that they push against the sides of its snout. This orientation ensures that water runs off the tilted shell, down the arched neck and twisted forelimbs, and puddles around the snout, which the tortoise pushes into the sand; it sucks up water from the small puddle that forms around the snout. The Aldabra Giant Tortoise lives on a coral atoll, where fresh water quickly drains away into the porous coral. It must drink water quickly from small, water-filled cavities, and so has developed special adaptations in the bony nasal passage that allow it to drink rapidly through the nostrils without water draining into the lungs.

Chelonians possess a cloacal bursa, a small sac that arises off the side of the cloaca, and in which water is stored. This forms a water reservoir for the tortoise, upon which it depends in times of drought. The water can be used for other purposes: during nesting the female often uses the water to soften the soil as she constructs the nest chamber; in sandy soils the moisture also binds the sand, allowing a deep chamber to be constructed without collapsing as it would with dry sand; in defence, tortoises can also void their cloacal water when handled. This may be effective with small predators, but it comes at a cost in times of drought, when the tortoise needs to conserve water.

Terrapins rarely suffer a water deficit, but many retain cloacal bursae for storing the water needed by females to construct nests. When submerged, many soft-shelled terrapins rhythmically fill the throat with water. Skin folds in the pharynx are rich in blood vessels, allowing for oxygen exchange in much the same way as the gills of fish.

An Australian terrapin (*Rheodytes leukops*) even has a cloacal 'gill'. It sucks water in and out of the cloacal bursa and absorbs oxygen from the water via the rich blood supply to the cloacal walls.

Floating giants

The Leopard Tortoise regularly enters small ponds, where it bobs like a bottle cork in the water. Its large, domed shell has a sizable lung space that imparts buoyancy. Smaller species, such as Padlopers and Tent tortoises, have very reduced lung spaces, and therefore low buoyancy, and many of these species sink when placed in water. This means that permanent rivers may limit their range: the Serrated Tortoise, for instance, does not occur south of the Orange River, whilst the Speckled Padloper does not occur north of the Orange River.

Thanks to its very large, but light, domed shell, the Aldabra Giant Tortoise floats even more impressively. In 2004 a tortoise washed ashore on the Tanzanian coast, having survived the long drift from Aldabra Atoll. The weak and starving tortoise was covered in barnacles, and must have been drifting at sea for a long time. The ability to float saved not only this individual, but has also saved the species from extinction. During previous Ice Ages, as sea levels rose and fell, the Aldabra coral atoll repeatedly emerged from and disappeared beneath the Indian Ocean. When sea levels rose and the atoll was submerged in water, all land life, including tortoises, were drowned. Fortunately, sea currents sweep north from Madagascar past the atoll. Giant tortoises swept out to sea following floods on Madagascar could have survived a month bobbing in gentle seas and, if lucky, been washed ashore like reptilian Robinson Crusoes. Fossils in the nooks and crannies of Aldabra reveal that Giant tortoises from Madagascar recolonised the atoll each time it re-emerged. Giant tortoises became extinct on Madagascar soon after people colonised it about 1 000 years ago. European seafarers soon decimated other tortoise populations on accessible islands, such as those of the Seychelles and Reunion. Only on the inaccessible atoll of Aldabra, which lacked game or fresh water to attract sailing ships, did the giants survive.

Leopard Tortoise swimming in a rock pool.

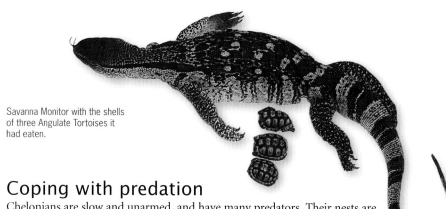

Savanna Monitor with the shells of three Angulate Tortoises it had eaten.

Coping with predation

Chelonians are slow and unarmed, and have many predators. Their nests are opened by common predators such as jackal, mongoose and monitor lizard. Chelonians' hard shells are effective in both size and strength, but only when fully formed. The shells of hatchlings and young chelonians are relatively soft, and easily crushed; the young therefore depend on secretive behaviour to avoid predation, but are still eaten by large birds such as storks, herons and ground hornbills, large monitor lizards, and even impaled on thorn bushes by butcher birds (fiscal shrikes). An adult tortoise's armour makes it a 'hard nut to crack'. However, some birds have learnt to break open the shell by dropping tortoises onto rocks. Crows, ravens, gulls and eagles have all learnt this technique. Smashed tortoise shells have been found beneath black eagle nests in the Karoo, whilst kelp gulls on Dassen Island on the Cape west coast kill many small tortoises. This is not a recently learnt approach: according to legend, the Greek poet, Aeschylus, was killed when an eagle dropped a tortoise on his head – some 2 500 years ago. Perhaps it was justified revenge for poor poetry – but it is more likely that it was an unfortunate accident as the eagle was preparing for a small meal.

Reproduction

All chelonians lay eggs: usually soft-shelled in aquatic forms (sea turtles, side-necked terrapins), but hard-shelled for tortoises and soft-shelled terrapins. The female takes great care in finding a suitably moist yet sunny spot in which to lay her eggs. She digs a small vertical pit with her hind legs, and after laying her eggs, covers them and leaves them to incubate. This is the extent of maternal care; after hatching, the young must fend for themselves. The time period between laying and hatching varies from 3 to 15 months and is, in part, dependent on the season. The chelonian egg has the unusual ability of entering a condition called diapause, during which embryonic development slows. Eggs laid in autumn undergo very little embryonic development during winter, and do not hatch much earlier than those laid the following spring.

Clutch size varies with the species, the greatest numbers being laid by sea turtles. They may lay over 800 eggs in a season, usually in multiple clutches (3–7) of 50–120 eggs. However, females generally breed only at intervals of 3–4 years. The largest African tortoises, the Leopard and Spurred tortoises, are similarly fecund, and females may lay 50–70 eggs per year, also in multiple clutches during a season. This contrasts with that of many smaller African tortoises and terrapins, which lay a single clutch per season, rarely exceeding 10 eggs. At the other extreme, many of the smaller endemic African tortoises, such as the Angulate Tortoise, Boulenger's Padloper and the Pancake Tortoise, lay only a single-egg clutch, although they may lay

4–6 eggs per year. This seems counterintuitive, as it suggests that the larger species suffer higher mortality rates; however, this may possibly be true, as the larger species have a longer period of growth before sexual maturity is reached, and may need to compensate for accumulative mortality incurred during this extended period.

Surprisingly, all chelonians still lay eggs, and no lineage has ever become live-bearing. Aquatic species, including terrapins and turtles, must brave the dangers presented by man, as well as by lesser predators, when they haul themselves ashore to lay their eggs.

Greater Padloper laying an egg.

Remarkably, this weakness has been circumvented by the unique reproductive behaviour of an Australian terrapin, *Chelodina rugosa*, which lays its eggs under water in soft mud, where they wait for the billabong to dry before undergoing development. The fully developed terrapins then wait in their egg chamber below the dried mud until the rains come and the water returns, whereupon they dig up through the mud and swim free.

For many chelonians, the sex of the embryo depends on the temperature at which the egg is incubated. At high temperatures (31–34°C), females are formed; males hatch from eggs incubated at lower temperatures. Nests in sunny positions produce more females than those laid in the shade. Climate change threatens to skew the natural sex ratios of many chelonians.

Angulate Tortoise hatching.

Boulenger's Padloper basking next to its rock shelter.

Dormancy – waiting for the good times

Many chelonians are faced with problematic periods when food, water and warmth – perhaps all at the same time – may be in short supply. Sea turtles may migrate to areas where conditions are more favourable, but this is not an option for slow-moving terrapins and tortoises. At such times they may simply hunker down and wait it out; where warmth or food are seasonal, they may go into a period of aestivation, hiding in burrows or under rock slabs or tucking themselves into thick vegetation.

Many terrapins inhabit temporary pans and marshes that regularly dry up. Then they burrow down into the moist soil, or into deep leaf litter, and wait for the rains to return. Unlike some sea turtles or North American terrapins, African species are not known to lie dormant under water. During aestivation, they undergo a number of physiological adjustments, including a reduction in heart rate and blood circulation. Before becoming dormant, the gut is usually emptied of all food and waste to avoid bacterial infections.

Conservation

With the exception of sea turtles, nearly all of Africa's chelonians are endemic. Among these, only two tortoises, the Geometric and the Spurred tortoises, are considered endangered. The Geometric Tortoise is among the world's most threatened species: only about 4 000 individuals survive. It occurs in low densities (between two and three tortoises per ha) in small pockets of coastal renosterveld in South Africa. Only 5 per cent of this habitat remains; the rest has been turned into wheat fields, vineyards and urban sprawl.

Throughout the world, sea turtle populations are threatened (and all seven species are listed on *CITES Appendix I*; most are listed as Endangered in the *IUCN Red List*, whilst two species, Kemp's Ridley and the Hawksbill, are considered Critically Endangered). Many turtles are slaughtered for meat as they come ashore to nest; others are inadvertently drowned in shrimp nets or killed on fishery longlines, or they choke on swallowed plastic sheeting.

Tortoise villages

The French non-governmental organisation SOPTOM, a world leader in chelonian conservation, started as the very successful 'Tortoise Village' at Gonfaron in southern France, which was initiated to protect the endangered Hermann's Tortoise, *Testudo hermanni*. (http://www.villagetortues.com).

Following on the success of this venture, similar 'villages' have been initiated at Noflaye (Senegal) and Ifaty (Madagascar). By empowering and educating local communities, these villages make a very real contribution to chelonian conservation – in sharp contrast with the 'official' national and international listing of endangered species, which are backed by very little protection on the ground.

Surprisingly, to date no similar social projects have been initiated for other threatened African chelonians – neither for the Pancake Tortoise in Tanzania nor, especially, for the Geometric Tortoise and the other endemic species in the Cape region of South Africa.

Sign at Tortoise Village in Noflaye, Senegal, where the Spurred Tortoise is protected.

Threats

Worldwide, chelonians face numerous threats, and their numbers are declining. The following short summary only brushes the surface of the topic, and emphasises African examples.

Bushmeat

People in Africa are becoming increasingly urbanised. In addition, there is a growing network of roads to previously isolated places, often built to support the extraction of timber. Fast transport and expanding markets mean that exploitation of tortoises for meat is increasing in many areas, especially as tribal taboos break down and human population levels place pressure on more traditional protein sources, such as fish and game. Tortoises have always been exploited by humans. Chelonian bones and shell fragments occur frequently in archaeological sites and, even today, the last vestiges of hunter-gatherer communities, such as the San of the Kalahari and the Hadza of Tanzania, consume tortoises and use the larger shells as vessels. Among the San, however, the taboo against eating tortoise meat, except by the very young and old, enforces a simple conservation measure that prevents overexploitation of an easily collected food resource. More recently, the bushmeat trade, including tortoises, has become a commercial venture in the hands of greedy people with no interest in sustainable use. Of

Pieces of meat from a butchered Aubrey's Flap-shelled Terrapin for sale in Gabon.

the numerous populations of giant tortoises that existed on Madagascar and the other islands of the Indian Ocean, only those on the inaccessible Aldabra Atoll survive.

Populations on the accessible islands – the Seychelles, Mauritius, and Réunion – are mainly extinct. They were decimated for food supplies, mainly by whaling ships at the end of the 19th century, when sailors collected this 'canned meat', which could simply be stored on deck, and butchered at weekly intervals on long sea voyages.

The new prosperity of China has led to a massive demand for tortoises in that country, both for pets and as food. Many Asian terrapins have become endangered within the last 15 years, and face extinction unless cultural eating habits can be changed. In 1996, 3.5 million kg of chelonians were imported and consumed in Hong Kong alone. From 2000–2003, nearly one million chelonians of 157 species were recorded in a survey of the turtle trade in Hong Kong, Shenzhen and Guangzhou, southern China. Seventy-two globally threatened species were traded, including 13 classified by the IUCN as Critically Endangered, 29 as Endangered, and 30 as Vulnerable. Enforcement of regulations controlling the trade in threatened species was limited, and globally threatened Asian species remained in trade in Hong Kong without the relevant licences. The economic boom that is fuelled by emerging markets in Asia puts tremendous pressure on world wildlife resources, as populations of local wildlife become extinct. Unless quickly protected, many Asian species will become extinct in the next few decades.

Habitat loss

The loss of land to farming or urban growth affects many chelonians. Much of the natural habitat for tortoises in the southwestern Cape, particularly that for the Geometric Tortoise, has been cleared for wheat fields and vineyards. There is little natural vegetation left in this 'global biodiversity hotspot'. The most pervasive effects of habitat loss are less obvious. One of the major threats to tortoises is the increasing frequency of fire. Large tracts of African savannah, particularly the miombo woodland belt, from northern Mozambique through to Angola, are deliberately burnt each year to promote grazing for cattle, to reduce undergrowth, or simply to improve visibility and easy walking. Many other fires occur through carelessness or neglect from discarded cigarettes or uncontrolled campfires. Tortoises are killed both directly and indirectly when they lose their food plants and shelters. The wetland habitats of terrapins are also facing numerous threats – siltation from erosion due to over-grazing, pollution with pesticides, eutrophication from fertiliser run-off, waterways clogged with alien plants, or simply wetlands drained for agricultural use.

Fire – the greatest danger

In January 2000 a fire started alongside a main road near the West Coast National Park in South Africa and swept into an area heavily infested with alien vegetation, where it burnt fiercely for several days. Strong, fast fires in sandy habitats such as this are the most dangerous for tortoises. The approaching fire cannot be outrun and there are few retreats, such as rocky outcrops, hollow logs or animal burrows, in which to escape. In total, the fire destroyed some 18 400 ha of habitat. Approximately 100 ha of the burnt area were surveyed 14 weeks after the fire, and 1 459 Angulate Tortoises were found; of these, only 99 were still alive (a mere 6.8 per cent).

A Geometric Tortoise that was killed by fire.

Other dead animals included small antelope (steenbok and duiker), mole rats, mice, ostriches, snakes, legless lizards and numerous invertebrates. Many small dead tortoises would not have been counted, their bodies being either covered in sand or burnt completely to ash.

Overall, a density of 15.4 tortoises per ha was found. When this is extrapolated to the total area burnt, it is conservatively estimated that between 99 000 and 282 000 Angulate Tortoises were killed in this single wildfire! This probably represents 10 times more tortoises than have ever been collected for research or illegally smuggled from South Africa for the pet trade. The disaster emphasises the need for greater habitat protection.

lectric fences

/ith the development of ecotourism and the :oliferation of game farms and wildlife reserves, rge tracts of land are encircled in electric fences ⸱ control the movement of mammals, particularly ckal, porcupine and warthog. The natural defensive ⸱haviour of tortoises – to retreat into their shells hen threatened – is ineffective when they come into ⸱ntact with electric fences.

Although single shocks are not fatal, continual ⸱cles of shocks incapacitate the tortoise until it is ⸱ally cooked alive in its shell. Large, reproductively ⸱tive females are particularly vulnerable. The ⸱oblem is not insurmountable: well designed ⸱nces can substantially reduce this carnage; they ⸱e just more expensive to install.

This Leopard Tortoise was electrocuted by an electric fence.

Pet trade

Tortoises do make endearing pets, and the emotive pull of a child's desire to own one is very difficult to resist. But tortoises are demanding pets, and although they can withstand great neglect, their climatic requirements are onerous. Most captives die within a year, from cold, lack of sunshine, or illness brought on by stress. It is difficult to appreciate the numbers of tortoises that are involved in the international pet trade. Between 1989 and 1997, nearly 500 000 non-indigenous terrapins and tortoises were imported into the USA. Over 75 000 of these were from Africa, mainly Bell's and Home's Hinged tortoises, and the Leopard Tortoise; most of these African tortoises came from Tanzania or Togo.

Alien introductions

A number of exotic species have been introduced to the African mainland. The American Red-eared Terrapin, *Trachemys scripta*, is the most exploited reptile in the world; over two million are exported each year from the USA for the international pet trade. Many are released into the wild when they become too large to keep or their owners get bored with them. Introduced populations have become established in many European countries, in Israel, Taiwan and elsewhere. The species has occasionally been released into Africa (Gambia and South Africa) but fortunately no breeding populations have become established. Importation is now banned in many countries, because of the danger of them escaping into the wild. They may also be a health hazard, as they can transmit disease-causing bacteria (*Salmonella* and *Arizona*).

The Aldabra Giant Tortoise, *Aldabrachelys gigantea*, has been introduced into Zanzibar where a population lives in a reserve on the main island.

An alien American Red-eared Terrapin.

Killed by kindness

People find tortoises endearing, perhaps because they are harmless and we can get up close and admire them. They are undeniably strange creatures, boxed in bone and trundling through space and time. They seem to epitomise age, and thus wisdom, in a homely, 'grandpa-ish' sort of way. This is probably why so many people, on seeing a tortoise on a road, feel compelled to stop and rescue it – to take it home and care for it, 'save' it in a strange garden with inquisitive pets, and daisies and marigolds for supper. Then, when the initial kindness and enthusiasm wanes, and when the garden flowerbeds begin to suffer, they are released into a strange place, in an unsuitable habitat or climate, where they are doomed to a slow death.

Zoos, snake parks and nature conservation departments are plagued with donations from well-meaning people of 'rescued' tortoises. These animals cannot be released into the wild; they may carry diseases that could infect local populations. They may also have different genetic heritages that, if released into a new area, could mix with those of the local tortoises, thus compromising the unique evolution of populations adapted to specific habitats.

More tortoises are probably 'killed by kindness' than are flattened by trucks on the roads. If you see a tortoise on the road, by all means stop and rescue it from danger. But please *release it immediately* in the veld beside the road and leave it in its true place – in the wild.

A young Leopard Tortoise crossing a tar road, from where it might be 'rescued'.

Tortoises

Tortoises

Tortoises belong to the family Testudinidae. They are found in the temperate and tropical regions of all continents except Australia. They also occur on Madagascar and other Indian Ocean islands, and the Galapagos Islands. Africa has the richest diversity of tortoises in the world. Seventeen genera, and possibly as many as 58 species, are found worldwide. Current debate centres on whether the many races and populations of Mediterranean tortoises (*Testudo*)

Kalahari Tent Tortoise.

should be treated as full species, and whether more than one species of Giant tortoise survives on the Indian Ocean islands. No fewer than 18 species in seven genera occur in sub-Saharan Africa. South Africa, despite its southerly position and mainly temperate climate, has more tortoise species than any other country in the world – 13 species in five genera. Two species, the African Spurred Tortoise and the Leopard Tortoise, are among the world's largest tortoises, exceeded in size only by a few giants living on isolated islands, such as the Aldabra Atoll and Galapagos Islands. In contrast, the Speckled Padloper, the world's smallest tortoise, lives among the floral wealth of South Africa's Namaqualand.

Tortoises are chelonians highly modified for terrestrial life. Most have domed, thick shells, except for the Pancake Tortoise from East Africa and, to a lesser degree, the Nama Padloper from southern Namibia, which have reduced and very thin shells. The top of the head is covered with several distinct shields. Their hind feet are elephant-like, and they walk on the tips of the claws of their heavily armoured forefeet. Buttock tubercles are often present. Mating is fairly typical in all species, with the male circling the female and occasionally ramming her with his shell until mounting is permitted. This is usually accompanied by much gaping and wheezing by the male.

The earliest Testudinidae fossils are from the Late Palaeocene of Mongolia. Older, possibly ancestral fossils are known from the Upper Cretaceous of Asia. Testudinid fossils occur in both Europe and North America in the Early Eocene, and by the Late Eocene they occur in North Africa (*Gigantochersina ammon*, from Egypt), indicating that, if tortoises did originate in Asia, they must soon have dispersed to other continents. Once in Africa, tortoises radiated rapidly and the continent became a major centre of diversification.

Recent molecular studies into DNA sequences indicate that there are at least three separate lineages endemic to Africa. The first comprises the Pancake Tortoise (*Malacochersus*), and the second the Hinged Tortoises (*Kinixys*); the third contains all the remaining tortoises that are found in southern Africa, including the Padlopers (*Homopus*), the Angulate Tortoise (*Chersina*), the Tent Tortoises (*Psammobates*) and the Leopard Tortoise (*Stigmochelys*). The Spurred Tortoise (*Geochelone*) is related to Asian species.

Key to the African genera in the Testudinidae

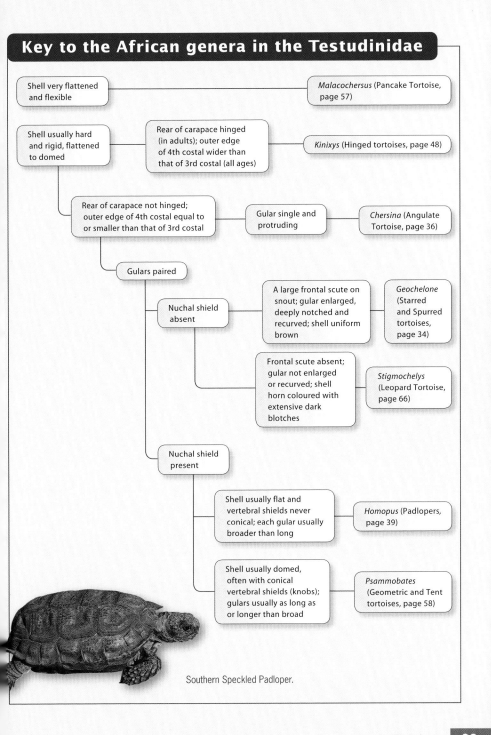

Shell very flattened and flexible → *Malacochersus* (Pancake Tortoise, page 57)

Shell usually hard and rigid, flattened to domed

Rear of carapace hinged (in adults); outer edge of 4th costal wider than that of 3rd costal (all ages) → *Kinixys* (Hinged tortoises, page 48)

Rear of carapace not hinged; outer edge of 4th costal equal to or smaller than that of 3rd costal

Gular single and protruding → *Chersina* (Angulate Tortoise, page 36)

Gulars paired

Nuchal shield absent

A large frontal scute on snout; gular enlarged, deeply notched and recurved; shell uniform brown → *Geochelone* (Starred and Spurred tortoises, page 34)

Frontal scute absent; gular not enlarged or recurved; shell horn coloured with extensive dark blotches → *Stigmochelys* (Leopard Tortoise, page 66)

Nuchal shield present

Shell usually flat and vertebral shields never conical; each gular usually broader than long → *Homopus* (Padlopers, page 39)

Shell usually domed, often with conical vertebral shields (knobs); gulars usually as long as or longer than broad → *Psammobates* (Geometric and Tent tortoises, page 58)

Southern Speckled Padloper.

Starred and Spurred Tortoises

Geochelone Fitzinger 1835

This is a large and ancient group, to which numerous living and fossil species have been assigned. Recently, the taxonomy has become very confused, and they have, at times, been divided into 7–8 living genera that are distinguished by subtle internal and skeletal characteristics, and high levels of genetic divergence. The re-assignment of fossils may require the discovery of more informative material. The genus name derives from the Greek (*geios* = of the earth, *chelone* = tortoise), and now contains only three living species, with one African and two Asian species. The African Spurred Tortoise is sometimes placed in its own genus (*Centrochelys*), but recent molecular studies have shown that it is closely related to the Indian Starred Tortoise (*Geochelone elegans*) and the Burmese Starred Tortoise (*G. platynota*).

African Spurred Tortoise

Geochelone sulcata (Miller 1779)

Other common name: **Crying Tortoise**

Named after the prominent growth rings (Latin *sulcus* = furrow, groove) in the shell scutes, and between the forked gulars.

Description The largest continental species, surpassed in size only by the giant island species from Aldabra and Galápagos. Indisputably the biggest African tortoise; males grow much larger (to 830 mm and 98 kg) than females (to only 60 kg). Captive specimens of over 100 kg are known; historically, wild specimens of well over 100 kg have been claimed. Their massive oval shells become straight-sided and more flattened dorsally. Female shell more domed than the flat-topped male shell. Obvious cervical notch but no nuchal scale. Usually 11 marginals a side; all, except those in the bridge, are serrated and those at the rear are upturned. All scutes have deep growth rings. Abnormally shaped scutes occur in over 8% of hatchlings. Plastron with a deep anal notch; thick, forked gulars at the front project forward under the neck. Bridge wide, with 2 axillaries and 2 inguinals. Head heavy with large scales and a weakly hooked upper jaw. Head, limbs and tail all brown. Forelimbs covered with large, knobbly, overlapping scales. 2–3 large, conical buttock tubercles, and large, conical, spur-like bony tubercles on the heel. Carapace uniformly brown; plastron and bridge cream or yellow. Hatchlings yellow to tan, with rounded, serrated shells.

African Spurred Tortoise.

Subspecies Although no subspecies have yet been described, significant genetic variation between western, central and eastern populations has been documented.

Habitat Restricted to arid savannah and scrubland in the Sahel region, with rainfall of 200–800 mm and in association with Sahelo-Sudanian vegetation.

Distribution Previously found continuously throughout the Sahel belt along the southern edge of the Sahara, from Senegal to Ethiopia. Now found

Heavily scaled forefeet of the African Spurred Tortoise.

only in isolated populations, from Ethiopia and Sudan westward through the dry regions of Chad, Niger and Mali to southern Mauritania and Senegal. A millennium ago the Sahel extended further north, and the range of the tortoise was much greater, but increasing desertification and human growth in the region has reduced and fragmented the range. Now extinct in the western Sahara.

Biology Because of the highly seasonal rainfall and vegetation growth in their range, much of their moisture is derived from their food. Most activity occurs during the rainy season (July–October), usually at dusk or dawn. In the

African Spurred Tortoise populations occur in Senegal.

dry season activity is very reduced, although short movements (100–200 m) may be made, usually at night. Adults excavate deep, long burrows on dunes or gravelled ground, which may be over 30 m long and 15 m deep. Many burrows are shared with other animals, such as snakes or monitor lizards. The burrows remain cool and moist, and are used when the tortoises aestivate during the dry season. Until they are about 5–7 years old, juveniles use old mammal burrows, which several tortoises may share. Mating starts just before the rains, and continues throughout the rainy season. A female may spend up to 2 days digging a nest hole. She first creates a shallow pit, about the size of her shell, by pushing soil away with her front and hind limbs, and digs the egg chamber

(about 15–20 cm wide and 20–30 cm deep) with her hind feet. After laying her eggs, she tamps down a layer of damp soil over the eggs, then fills the rest of the chamber, levelling the whole nest area to hide the location of the chamber. Eggs are laid at the end of the rainy season, usually in 2–3 (up to 4) clutches. Natural incubation of clutches in Chad took 144–149 days, but incubation in captivity is quicker (90–101 days). The emergence of hatchlings may be delayed until the rains return. They do not emerge until the yolk sac is completely reabsorbed. Clutches comprise 13–31 (average 19) white, spherical, hard-shelled eggs (37–45 mm, 32–70 g) with brittle shells. Hatchlings weigh about 50 g, and growth is rapid. Within 9 months juveniles may weigh over 200 g, and 3-year-old juveniles weigh about 4 kg. Sexual maturity is reached in about 10 years in females (15 in males). Succulent plants and grasses are the preferred food. There are many predators, particularly monitor lizards, on hatchlings and juveniles, but adults are threatened only by man, fire and drought.

They are long-lived, with reports of individuals living over 100 years. Very large adults are revered by Dogon communities in Mali, and considered to represent the spirits of the ancestors; flat-topped old males are coddled in captivity, and serve as living thrones from which chiefs pass judgement in tribal disputes.

> **CONSERVATION** Included on the *2007 IUCN Red List* as Vulnerable. The fragmented populations are all in decline, threatened by both habitat loss and competition for food with human livestock. In addition, many are kept in captivity, both internationally and locally. In much of the Sahel region the tortoise is considered a lucky charm and a symbol of longevity and fecundity. It is believed that more tortoises are now kept in captivity than occur in the wild. To promote the species' conservation and generate captive progeny for release into protected areas, the 'S.O.S. Sulcata' programme was initiated in 1993. 'Tortoise villages' and educational and breeding centres have been developed at both Sangalkam and Noflaye, Senegal.

Angulate Tortoise

Chersina   Gray 1831

These tortoises are endemic to the tip of southern Africa. They are unique among African tortoises in having an undivided gular at the front of the plastron. Known from a single living species; an unnamed fossil species (see page 8), from middle Pliocene (4.0–4.5 Ma) deposits on the Western Cape coast, awaits description. The name derives from Greek (*chersinos* = land tortoise).

Angulate Tortoise

Chersina angulata   (Schweigger 1812)

Other common names: **Bowspit Tortoise, Fighting Tortoise**

Named after the elongate, angular (Latin *angulus* = angle, corner) gular scute that projects forward beneath the head of adult males, and perhaps the marginal colour pattern.

Description A medium-sized tortoise, larger in the western regions. In the east, males rarely exceed 220 mm (1 kg). On Dassen Island and the adjacent Western Cape mainland even females may exceed 240 mm (1.5 kg) and males may exceptionally reach 300 mm. Carapace elongate and flared at the front and back in mature males; more domed in females, particularly toward the rear. Scutes slightly raised. 10–12 (usually 11) marginals. Nuchal present. Single gular protrudes beneath the head in mature males. Beak weakly hooked, bicuspid or

Shells of male (left) and female (right) Angulate Tortoises.

Male Angulate Tortoise.

tricuspid, and rarely serrated. Five claws on each forefoot. Buttock tubercles absent. Tail does not have a terminal spine. Carapace scutes light straw yellow with dark brown areolae and black edges. Marginals have a black triangle on the posterior edges. Plastron with dark, irregular centre, often with white sutures in old animals. Abdominals light orange to red, varying seasonally, and possibly linked to a diet rich in carotene. These individuals are particularly colourful (the 'rooipens' form) and are common in the Western Cape.

Shell of old adults smooth and a uniform dirty straw colour. Unlike most other African tortoises, males grow larger than females, and have a 'peanut' shell shape, an elongate gular, longer tail and a deep plastral concavity. Hatchling carapace is flat, with a greater curved width than curved length, but with growth, the shape changes rapidly to adult ratios.

Habitat Varied, including sandy coastal regions and coastal fynbos in the west, and mesic thicket in the east. Isolated inland populations inhabit moister karroid habitats associated with higher rainfall.

Distribution Mainly restricted to South Africa. Found in the Cape coastal region from East London to the Orange River valley, extending inland as far as Cradock in association with Karoo broken veld. Isolated records in southern Namibia, and relict populations in moister regions of the Karoo escarpment. Introduced to two offshore islands – Dyer's and Dassen islands – in the last century.

Biology The diet includes grasses, annuals and succulents. Angulate tortoises drink through the nose from rock pools; on sandy soils they push the snout into the soil, and, with rear legs and necks extended, drink the water that runs off the shell to form a puddle around the head. They can withstand body temperatures up to 40°C, but prefer to be cooler (around 30°C). Never active at temperatures below 14°C, and rarely above 29°C. In late spring and summer they are active in the morning and evening, displaying bimodal activity and sheltering at midday. At other times they are active throughout the day.

Populations reach their highest densities on islands (for instance, Dassen Island) or at habitat ecotones that offer vegetation for cover and open areas for foraging, basking and nesting sites. Densities of up to 34 tortoises per ha may occur. Individuals have lived for up to 32 years in captivity.

Predators include small carnivores, baboons, rock monitors, secretary birds, sea gulls and crows. Hatchlings have even been found skewered on tree thorns by fiscal shrikes.

They readily eject the liquid contents of the bowels when handled, often spraying it some distance.

Males and females may have similar-sized home ranges (up to 2 ha, but often less in moister habitats). Juveniles wander slowly from place to place, and select a suitable territory only when they reach maturity.

Although living in high densities, males do not defend territories. Instead, dominant males prevent other males from mating with females. Combat between males involves vigorous ramming and use of the enlarged gular to overturn the opponent. A single 'fall' may not resolve the dispute. Battles may be fierce, as breeding males try to flip one another over – so mature males develop a low, peanut-shaped shell that flares at the front and back, lowering the centre of gravity, and making them difficult to overturn. As tortoise mating is usually prolonged and noisy, it is not easy for sneaky, subordinate males to mate without being spotted. Access to females depends upon victory in combat, and larger males usually win fights. As a result, males grow larger than females (in most other tortoise species, the female is larger).

After rain, when the soil is soft and moist, the female digs a shallow depression about 100 mm wide, and within it a smaller chamber 40 mm wide and deep. She uses the claws of her hind feet to break up the soil, which she then pushes away with the side of her lower leg. She lays a single hard-shelled, spherical egg (30–35 x 37–42 mm, 20–25 g), very rarely 2. After laying, she tamps down the soil with her shell. The whole procedure may take 2–3 hours. Although the area is carefully camouflaged, many eggs are excavated and eaten by mongooses.

Incubation takes 90–200 days, depending on the season. Eggs may crack 6–10 days before young emerge. Hatchlings weigh 8–12 g and are 32–35 mm long. Growth is rapid in the first 8–10 years, slowing thereafter, with little growth after 20 years. Sexual maturity is reached in 9–12 years. Most eggs are laid within 3 days after rainfall; in dry periods, eggs may be retained for up to 212 days before being laid. Females prepare a new egg for development immediately after nesting; they may lay an egg up to 6 times a year.

There are many unusual features in Angulate Tortoise biology; males fight and grow larger than females; females lay only a single egg and have a protracted breeding season. These behaviours may be linked in an ecological interplay between predation and reproductive behaviour. Tortoises suffer high nest predation, as mongoose and jackal dig up nests and eat the hatchlings. In response, female tortoises may not 'put all their eggs in one basket', and instead lay single eggs at frequent intervals. Females must then have a protracted breeding season, and may be receptive to mating for longer periods. Bigger, more aggressive males can dominate these additional mating opportunities.

> **CONSERVATION** Not considered threatened, as they occur at very high densities in many areas. Livestock farming may have led to population increases in some areas, such as the Eastern Cape, due to the eradication of jackal, mongoose and other predators, and the creation of cleared areas in thicket habitats.

Angulate Tortoise in dune thicket habitat at Kini Bay, near Port Elizabeth.

Padloper Tortoises

Homopus Duméril and Bibron 1835

Also called Cape tortoises, the genus is endemic to southern Africa and restricted mainly to the Cape, with two species occurring in adjacent regions. There are five living species, with one fossil species (*H. fenestratus*) from unknown strata, described from Carlisle Bridge near Grahamstown, South Africa.

It contains small to very small tortoises, including the world's smallest chelonian. The carapace is not hinged and is relatively flat, with the scutes never raised into knobs, and often with depressed centres. The plastron has paired, thickened gulars that are wider than they are long. A nuchal is present. Shell abnormalities (extra and misshapen scutes, etc.) are relatively common. The genus is named after the similarity between the front and hind feet of two species (Greek *homo* = alike, *pous* = foot, meaning 'same foot'), both of which have 4 claws (all other tortoises, including other Padlopers, have 5 claws on the front feet, making it something of a misnomer). In all Padloper species females grow larger than males, and have deeper shells.

Parrot-beaked Padloper

Homopus areolatus   (Thunberg 1787)

Other common names: **Beaked Tortoise, Beaked Cape Tortoise, Common Padloper**

Named after the areolae (dimpled centres, Latin *areolatus* = with small spaces) on the vertebral and costal scutes.

Description A small tortoise, averaging 100–130 mm in length (females to 160 mm). Shell lacks a hinge, has a nuchal and paired gulars; often attractively sculptured, with scute margins deeply etched and centres indented. Usually 11 marginals. Beak strongly hooked (hence the common name), tricuspid, with a weakly serrated edge. Nostrils situated high on the snout, which is often swollen. Each forelimb has 4 claws, and covered with very large, overlapping scales. Buttock tubercles absent or very small in both sexes. Tail lacks a terminal spine. Mature males have long tails, but no plastral concavity. Females grow slightly larger than males. Carapace yellowish olive to green, usually with red-brown areolae and dark brown to black margins in juveniles and adult females; males remain uniform orange-brown, except for a greenish tinge to the edges of the vertebral and costal scutes, and develop bright orange swollen nasal scales in the breeding season.

Bright swollen nasal scales in male Parrot-beaked Padloper.

Male Parrot-beaked Padloper with orangish shell.

Female Parrot-beaked Padloper with greenish shell.

Fynbos habitat near Port Elizabeth.

Plastron yellowish with a brown centre.
Habitat Varied: coastal fynbos, karroid broken veld and open mesic thicket.
Distribution Endemic to South Africa, mainly in the Cape coastal region from King William's Town to Klawer, extending inland to Pearston in the east and Middelpos in the Roggeveldberge. Occurs below 600 m, but extends inland to higher altitudes via the moist corridor of the Cradock gap.

Biology Due to their small size these tortoises rarely forage in the open, favouring sunny spots around the edge of thick cover. Often shelter under rocks, in grass tussocks or in disused animal burrows; can easily climb up steep slopes. Struggle vigorously when restrained, alternatively hooking each forelimb backwards; will readily void the contents of their cloacal water reservoir. Eaten by crows and even secretary birds. They have lived for longer than 28 years in captivity. Males fight frequently and aggressively and can inflict severe bites on each other. Combat between males involves each biting the anterior edge of the other's carapace and then pushing against one another, sometimes for over an hour. Subordinate or defeated males are pursued, with the dominant male attempting to bite the retreating male. Females are gravid from May to November, and lay a clutch of 1–3 eggs (rarely 4) in a small nest hole dug in sandy soil. Some females may lay an additional clutch in a season. The eggs are relatively small, elongate and oval (27–33 x 20–23 mm), and take 150–300 days to hatch. The young weigh 4–8 g and measure 30 mm.

CONSERVATION Widespread in the southern Cape region; rarely common, but there is no evidence of significant population declines. Recorded from numerous protected areas, such as the Addo Elephant, Bontebok and West Coast national parks, and is consequently not considered threatened.

Karoo Padloper

Homopus femoralis Boulenger 1888

Other common name: **Karoo Cape Tortoise**

Named for the large buttock tubercle that is found on the thigh (Latin *femur* = thigh).

Description A small tortoise but the largest Padloper, averaging 100–130 mm in length (females to 168 mm) and weighing 200–300 g. Shell lacking a hinge, with a nuchal, paired gulars, and usually 11 marginals. Beak not hooked, but tricuspid with a serrated edge. Nostrils below the level of the eye. Forelimbs covered with large, overlapping scales, and with 4 claws. Buttock tubercles present in both sexes, but may be small or absent in juveniles. Tail lacks a terminal spine. Carapace olive or reddish brown, with black margins to the scutes in juveniles. Plastron a uniform dirty yellow-green in adults, often with darker areas restricted to the anterior edge of the scutes in juveniles. Skin of the body yellow-brown, and sometimes orange-pink. Males have longer tails but no plastral concavity. Females grow larger than males.

Habitat Grasslands of mountain plateaus, particularly along the Karoo escarpment.

Distribution Largely endemic to South Africa, from the inland mountains of the Eastern Cape extending into southern and central Free State, Northern Cape around Kimberley, and the mountains of southeast Lesotho. Relict populations occur along the old escarpment edge in the Karoo, from Murraysburg to Sutherland, possibly into the northwest Little Karoo.

Biology Poorly known, although common in suitable habitat. They shelter under rock slabs or in animal burrows and old, hollow termite nests, and hibernate during winter, when snow may sporadically fall in much of their range. Enemies include crows and birds of prey, jackals and the rock monitor. The female lays 1–3 oval, hard-shelled eggs (29–35 x 25–27 mm) in summer. Hatchlings measure 25–30 mm and weigh 6–8 g.

> **CONSERVATION** It has the widest distribution of any Padloper. Favoured habitat (montane grassland) is extensively used for sheep farming, but there is no evidence of tortoise population declines due to farming. Recorded from a number of protected areas (for instance, the Karoo, Mountain Zebra and Camdeboo national parks); not currently threatened.

Head of Karoo Padloper.

he Karoo Padloper is largely endemic to South Africa.

Montane grassland habitat of the Karoo Padloper.

Boulenger's Padloper
Homopus boulengeri Duerden 1906

Other common names: **Boulenger's Cape Tortoise, Donderweerskilpad, Klipskilpad, Rooiskilpadjie**

Named in honour of the eminent herpetologist George Boulenger (1858–1937), who worked at the British Museum of Natural History and described the Karoo Padloper.

Description A small tortoise, averaging 100–130 mm (to 160 mm). Shell flattened, with a very rounded bridge, usually 12–13 marginals, and a nuchal that is longer than it is broad. Beak rounded, although it may appear bicuspid in aged specimens when the beak becomes worn. Each forelimb covered with very large, overlapping scales, and with 5 claws. Buttock tubercles present in most males, but usually absent in females. Tail lacks a terminal spine. Males have long tails and a deep concavity in the plastron. Carapace plain and varies in colour from dark red to yellow-brown, and sometimes pale olive. Plastron similar, but lighter in colour. Skin of the neck and limbs dull yellow, and sometimes bright yellow with orange scales.

Habitat Rocky areas in karroid regions, particularly dolerite ridges.

Distribution Endemic to the Great Karoo of South Africa, from Pearston in the east, Steytlerville in the south, Sutherland and Carnarvon in the west, extending into the western Little Karoo at Anysberg.

Biology This very secretive species shelters under rock slabs on rocky outcrops, plateaus and dolerite ridges. Active on cool summer days, particularly when thunderstorms threaten (hence the common Afrikaans name). Killed and eaten by crows, which break their shells by dropping them onto rocks. Breeding is poorly known. Females lay a single egg (32–39 x 22–23 mm, 10 g) at regular intervals during summer. The large, oblong egg is wider than the pelvic canal, necessitating softening of sutures at the rear of the shell during egg laying.

LEFT: Boulenger's Padloper has a rounded beak.

BELOW: This species has a flattened shell and the carapace is plain.

BELOW RIGHT: Typical rocky habitat of the Padloper.

CONSERVATION Rarely seen, but common in suitable habitat, with a wide distribution in the sparsely inhabited Great Karoo. Not known to be presently endangered, although it may be threatened by future climate change.

Speckled Padloper
Homopus signatus (Gmelin 1789)

Other common name: **Speckled Cape Tortoise**

Named after the intricate patterning of the carapace
(Latin *signum* = mark, seal).

Southern (left) and northern races of the Speckled Padloper.

Description The world's smallest tortoise, averaging only 80–90 mm (female to 96 mm). Shell flattened and straight-sided, with a nuchal as broad as it is long, that may appear almost divided. Bridge with a prominent ridge. Usually 12 marginals, serrated in the northern race and smooth in the southern. A single inguinal, and usually a single axillary. Dorsal scutes flat, sometimes even with depressed centres and deep, incised sutures. Males have relatively shorter plastrons than females to improve walking and tail movement during copulation. Serration of the marginals greater in juveniles and young adults, decreasing with age. Prefrontal on the snout usually elongate and longitudinally divided; beak usually bicuspid, with a serrated lateral edge. Each forelimb covered with large, overlapping scales, and with 5 claws. Buttock tubercle present in both sexes. Males have a well developed plastral concavity, and a long tail. Coloration varies geographically (see subspecies) and between the sexes. Females have darker shells with more rays and fewer speckles than males.

Subspecies Two races are recognised. The typical race, *H. s. signatus*, occurs in Namaqualand, with isolated records from the Richtersveld and Onseepkans. Shell usually tan (sometimes light orange) with extensive black splashes, and has serrated marginals; nuchal wider than it is long; carapace shields raised, with sunken centres. The southern race, *H. s. cafer*, occurs in the Western Cape from Piketberg to Klawer and Calvinia. Shell orange-red to salmon pink

Northern Speckled Padloper.

with fine black spots and stippling; marginals not serrated; nuchal narrower than it is long; carapace shields smooth.

Habitat Mainly restricted to the western succulent Karoo, but extending into fynbos in the south.

Distribution Endemic to South Africa, ranging from the Western Cape, north through

Rock outcrops and succulent Karoo habitat near Springbok.

Over 25 species of plant eaten; important food plants include *Oxalis* spp., *Leysera tenella*, *Grielum humifusum* and *Crassula thunbergiana minutiflora*. Succulents, such as *Crassula*, may also be a source of water. Male combat has been observed, but does not seem to be as frequent as in the Parrot-beaked Padloper. Mating takes place throughout spring and autumn, with head-bobbing between the sexes preceding copulation. Females lay a number of single-egg clutches (possibly 3–4) at 25-day to 43-day intervals, and are gravid from August to October. Most females (75%) reproduce each year. Larger females produce larger eggs. Growth is relatively slow (a maximum of 9.5 mm a year for juveniles); females with shells about 85 mm long are sexually mature. In captivity females may lay eggs when only 3.5 years old, but growth is much slower in the wild, where maturity is only reached after 11–12 years. In years of low rainfall growth is retarded, and tortoises may even shrink in size as bone and soft tissues are reabsorbed. The egg is the largest produced by any chelonian relative to its body size, measuring about 25 x 35 mm; this ensures that the hatchling is large, with sufficient food reserves to withstand the harsh droughts that affect the area. The egg is larger than the female's pelvic canal; the rear of the shell has to become flexible to allow its passage. It is laid in moist soil under an overhanging rock or vegetation, deep enough (at least 4 cm) to protect against desiccation or overheating. The large size of females allows them both to produce large eggs and to be able to dig nests deep enough to ensure successful development. The egg takes 100–120 days to hatch (at 30°C); the small hatchlings (carapace length 30 mm, weight 7 g) start to feed immediately.

Namaqualand to the southern bank of the Orange River valley.
Biology Active throughout the year, although more so during the wet winter than the dry summer season. Active in the early morning in rocky areas, foraging for small succulent plants among granite slabs. Common in suitable habitat; several may be found sheltering together under a rock slab. Feed selectively on the leaves and flowers of small herbaceous plants, geophytes and, to a lesser extent, grasses; may also take a few insects.

CONSERVATION Inhabits a sparsely populated semi-arid area; currently considered near-threatened, but predicted to be further threatened by extensive future climate change-induced habitat loss; its range is expected to contract by about 50% in the next few decades. The reproductive biology of the species is very specialised; long droughts may quickly retard growth and egg production in females, compounding habitat loss with low reproductive rates. The southern race is more immediately threatened, due to its restricted range and greater agricultural activity in the area. Both races are collected illegally for the international pet trade.

Nama Padloper

Homopus solus Branch, 2007

Other common names: **Namibian Cape Tortoise,
Nama Cape Tortoise**

Named after the lonely places it inhabits (Latin *solos* = lonely,
solitary) and in allusion to the desert sun (Latin *sol* = sun).

Description A very small tortoise, averaging 80–100 mm (female to 114 mm, male to 90 mm). Shell flattened, with a small, narrow nuchal, a well defined ridge on the bridge, 2 axillaries and a single inguinal, and usually 11 smooth marginals. Dorsal shell elements (neurals and pleurals) underlying the vertebrals and costals, reduced in size internally, leaving large gaps in the bones of the carapace in juveniles. These gaps are smaller but still present even in relatively large adults, making the shell soft and flexible. Each forelimb with 5 claws, and covered with very large, overlapping scales. Buttock tubercles absent in both sexes. Anal midline suture of the plastron longer than the femoral. Adult males have an obvious plastral concavity. Head has fragmented prefrontals; beak tricuspid with a serrated rear edge. Coloration relatively constant; carapace typically red-brown, often with an olive tinge in old adults. Each dorsal scute usually has a pale areola and a dark border that is normally rich mahogany red in colour and may be irregularly flecked. Plastron similarly patterned, although the dark border is often more extensive, particularly on the anterior and lateral margins. Ventral surface of mature males may become infused with darker blotches. Head and limbs pale to dirty brown. Very large females more uniform in coloration, with dark scute margins limited only to the sutures, and the dark margins of the plastron more blotched. Subadults pale brown with the dark brown borders very reduced and limited to the sutures.

Nama Padloper.

Nama Padloper has a typically red-brown carapace.

Pro-Namib habitat of the Nama Padloper near Aus, Namibia.

Habitat Barren mountains with sparse, succulent vegetation in the Namib Desert, and in grassland along the Aus escarpment. Populations in the Namib Desert near Lüderitz subject to extreme aridity, where yearly rainfall is often less than 10 mm. Rainfall at Aus is higher (80–100 mm annually), falling mainly from January to June; winter snowfalls are common.

Distribution Endemic to southern Namibia, with the main distribution centred around the escarpment mountains near Aus, extending 50 km north to the plateau of the Rooirand Mountains. Scattered records from the Kowiesberg near Lüderitz, and adjacent areas. The southern limit Witputs on the Huib Plateau near Rosh Pinah.

Biology A rock-living species, inhabiting granite outcrops in very arid terrain, although they may forage in sand gullies between rock outcrops. Usually shelter under westerly-facing rock slabs, but may rest under thorny bushes. Most active during and after winter rains. Their light, flexible shells allow them to climb steep rock faces but the reduction of bone in the shell may make them more susceptible to predation; they are shy and rarely seen. Home ranges are small; larger in males (0.74 ha) than females (0.17 ha). Males also make greater daily movements (average 50 m) than females (average 21 m). Inland they drink from rock pools, but coastal populations in the Namib Desert must obtain their moisture from their food or from the frequent fogs that occur in the region. They eat small annuals and succulents, and even graze lichens. In captivity mating occurs throughout the year, particularly after rain showers. The male pursues the female, shaking his head. During mating the male gapes his mouth wide. A single egg is laid at a time, usually in the afternoon and in a shallow hole (5–7 cm deep) dug beneath a rock overhang or vegetation. Most eggs are laid in the winter–spring period (July–October). The egg may measure from 26–30 x 36–41 mm and weigh about 2 g. A wild hatchling measured 32.5 mm, but captive hatchlings are slightly larger (average 36.2 mm). In captivity incubation of eggs took 87–123 days, and males reached sexual maturity in about 2 years.

CONSERVATION All tortoises are protected by national legislation in Namibia. Listed in the *2007 IUCN Red List of Threatened Species* as Vulnerable. Has a very restricted distribution and is poorly known. May be threatened by overgrazing by cattle, desertification, as well as illegal collecting for the international pet trade. Known to occur in a number of protected areas, including the National Diamond Coast Recreation Area and the Ai-Ais-Hunsberg Reserve.

Padloper Tortoise Shells

The shells of Padloper tortoises are beautifully sculpted and patterned. However, they are also often malformed, with additional vertebral and costal scutes.

Parrot-beaked Padloper

Boulenger's Padloper

Karoo Padloper

Speckled Padloper

Hinged Tortoises

Kinixys Bell 1827

These unusual tortoises have a unique hinge in the adult carapace
that allows the rear of the shell to close, protecting the hind feet and tail region.
The genus name derives from this unique feature (Greek *kineo* = to move, *ixys* = small
of the back). The hinge is not developed in juveniles. The latter look similar to Padlopers
(*Homopus* sp, page 39), but the ranges of the two genera do not overlap. Shells can be
distinguished by the outer edge of costal 3, which is longer than that of costal 4. The
hinge develops first at the edge between marginals 7 and 8, and then spreads inward,
separating costals 2 and 3, the bony sutures being replaced with fibrous cartilage. In
some species the hinge is weakly developed, even in adults. A nuchal is usually present.
The paired gulars are very thickened at the front; they are sometimes longer than they
are broad. There are usually 5 claws on each of the forefeet (except in one subspecies).
Females grow larger than males, except for the Forest Hinged Tortoise. Six species are
recognised. Two of these, the Forest and Home's Hinged tortoises, are restricted to the
rainforests of western and central Africa. The other four species inhabit savannah, mainly
in eastern and southern Africa, with one species entering West Africa.

Home's Hinged Tortoise

Kinixys homeana Bell 1827

Named in honour of the British anatomist
Sir Everard Home (1756–1832).

Description A medium-sized Hinged tortoise.
Shell elongated (to 223 mm); carapace flat-
topped, sometimes slightly keeled. Females
grow larger than males. Marginals (11–12)
large, serrated and flared at the front and
back, becoming almost recurved at the rear.
Back of the carapace drops abruptly at the last
vertebral. Elongate nuchal usually present; all
except the first vertebrals broader than they are
long. Each vertebral with a row of low, knob-
like projections which may form a weak keel
on juveniles, but is lost with age. Supracaudal
undivided and recurved. Hinge well developed.
Paired gulars thick, short, wide and notched,
and project only slightly beyond the shell.

2–4 small axillary scutes and a large inguinal,
which is in contact with the femoral scute. Rear
of the short plastron shallowly notched. Head
small, with a rounded snout and a hooked
upper jaw. Prefrontals divided longitudinally;
frontal large, may be subdivided. Other head
scales small and irregularly shaped. 5 claws on
each forefoot; front of the forelimb has 5–8 rows
of scattered, large overlapping scales. Buttock
tubercles absent; heel may have a large spur-like
scale. Tail ends in a claw-like tubercle. Carapace
varies from dark brown to tan, sometimes
with a vague radiating pattern of pale rays on
the costals and scattered dark patches along
the sutures. New growth between the costals

and marginals is often light yellow. Plastron dark brown to tan, with some yellow at the seams. Head brown with yellow on the crown and upper jaw. Limbs and tail brown to yellow. Breeding males develop a lighter head and a plastral concavity, although this is not as pronounced as in the Forest Hinged Tortoise. Hatchling carapace with very spiny margins and no hinge.

Habitat Humid lowland evergreen forest, along streams and around swampy areas.

Distribution Moist western African belt, from Liberia to Cameroon and the Congo. No confirmed records from Gabon.

Biology Poorly known, despite often being sold in the international pet trade. Bask, rarely, in sunny spots on the forest floor, and forage in shade. During the dry season they are less active, but they do not aestivate like savannah species. Omnivorous, feeding on a wide variety of food, particularly fungi, fruit and seeds, and invertebrates such as snails and isopods. Occasionally eat frogs and earthworms. The eggs are oval to almost spherical (46 x 35 mm) and have brittle shells. Incubation may take 5 months. Hatchlings are 42–47 mm long.

Lowland evergreen forest habitat of Home's Hinged Tortoise.

CONSERVATION The species is of conservation concern (Vulnerable, *IUCN 2007*), as large tracts of suitable habitat have been lost to agricultural developments and village clearings. In serious decline over much of its range, due mainly to habitat loss, intensive harvesting for subsistence, traditional medicine and the international pet trade.

An adult Home's Hinged Tortoise.

Forest Hinged Tortoise

Kinixys erosa (Schweigger 1812)

Other common names: **Eroded Hinge-back, Serrated Hingeback, Rosy Hingeback, Schweigger Hingeback**

Named for the jagged shell margin (Latin *erosus* = eaten away). Sadly, for other reasons, this is now an apposite name, as species numbers are in sharp decline due to unsustainable exploitation for bushmeat.

Adult Forest Hinged Tortoise.

Juvenile Forest Hinged Tortoise.

Head of an adult male Forest Hinged Tortoise.

Description The largest Hinged tortoise, reaching 400 mm in length. Males grow bigger than females. Shell elongated, with flat, unkeeled top and sloping sides. Marginals flared and recurved anteriorly, strongly serrated at the rear, forming a 'toothed skirt'. Shell slopes gently upward at the front, but drops off sharply at the rear (although not as abruptly as in Home's Hinged Tortoise). Nuchal usually absent; all vertebrals broader than they are long, particularly the last. 11–12 marginals; supracaudal undivided. Paired gulars thickened and notched, jutting forward beyond the carapace, especially in males. 3–4 small axillary scutes; 1 large inguinal that is in contact with the femoral. Plastral short, shallowly notched at the rear. Juvenile shell flattened, hingeless and spiny-edged. Head relatively small, with a rounded snout and a hooked upper jaw. Prefrontals divided longitudinally, large frontal may be subdivided, and the rest of the head scales are small and irregularly shaped. 4–5 longitudinal rows of large, sometimes overlapping scales on the front of the forelimb. 5 claws on each forefoot, but no buttock tubercles or spur-like enlarged scales on the heel. Tail ends in a claw-like tubercle, which is larger in males. Male with long, thick tail, more projecting gulars, and a well developed plastral concavity. Carapace plain dark brown, or dark brown with yellow to orange centres to the scutes. Lower edges of the costals often irregularly blotched in bright yellow. The plastron is dark brown to black with some yellow along the seams. The head in adult females usually yellow, brighter on the snout, but darker on the crown and neck. Adult males develop almost uniform whitish yellow heads. Limbs and tail yellow, darker toward the body.

Young carapace red-brown with yellow-edged scales. Plastron black-brown.

Habitat Primary forest, preferring moist areas, such as marshes, river banks and wetlands.

Distribution West Africa, from Gambia eastward to the DRC and Uganda, and south to Cabinda and southern Angola.

Biology Often found resting in water and swim well. On land, spend much time buried beneath roots, logs and plant debris. Omnivorous, feeding on plants, fruits, mushrooms, small invertebrates and carrion. Particularly fond of mushrooms and earthworms. Forage and mate at night; may undertake long journeys (up to 275 m). Home range about 2 ha, always including a water body. May spend several days resting in their retreats. Although adult males grow larger than females, male-male combat is rarely observed. Mating

Lowland forest habitat in the Central African Republic.

activity is observed throughout the year, and may occur at all hours of the day and night. Mating is an energetic affair, during which the male hisses, circles and rams the female, sometimes turning her on her back. Clutches of 1–5 oval, hard-shelled eggs are laid in the ground or simply covered with leaves and dead vegetation. Several clutches may be laid in a season. The eggs are relatively large, thick-shelled, weighing 17–28 g and measuring 35 mm x 45 mm. Incubation can be protracted (140–300 days), depending upon how much sun reaches the nest site.

> **CONSERVATION** Like Home's Hinged Tortoise, and for the same reasons, this species is of conservation concern. Habitat loss and unsustainable harvesting are causing serious population declines over much of its range, and although not currently included in the *2007 IUCN Red List of Threatened Species*, it is a likely candidate.

Bell's Hinged Tortoise
Kinixys belliana   (Gray 1831)

Other common names: **Eastern Hinged Tortoise (typical race), Western Hinged Tortoise (western race)**

Named after Thomas Bell (1792–1880), the British surgeon and zoologist, whose beautiful book, *A Monograph of the Testudinata* (1832–36), described all known chelonians, living and extinct.

Description A medium-sized tortoise (to 230 mm). Carapace elongate, domed, with a flat, sometimes slightly keeled top and sloping sides. The rear of the shell slopes, unlike the 'square-backed' shape of the forest species. Usually 11 marginals, those at the front are, at most, slightly flared, those at the rear not flared and only slightly serrated. Hatchlings without spiny shell or obvious hinge, although the latter is prominent in adults. Nuchal of varied shape – tiny, elongate or broad. Paired gulars less than twice as wide as they are long, not forked, and with a flat or convex lip. Supracaudal undivided, with a smooth underside. 2–4 small axillary scales; 1 large inguinal. Head small, with a rounded snout. Beak unicuspid; prefrontal large, and may be subdivided or longitudinally divided; other head scales small and irregularly shaped. Front of the forelimbs with large, overlapping, sometimes pointed scales, and with 5 claws (only 4 in the western African race). Buttock tubercles absent; tail with terminal spine, larger in males. Carapace coloration varied; in the east it has a tan and black radial pattern (4–6 thick rays) on the vertebrals and costals; in the west the pattern is more zonal, with the scutes having dark centres and rings of tan and black. The patterning may fade in adults, particularly in males. Plastron colour varies, but is largely black in juveniles, becoming cream with dark areas with age. Limbs and tail dull brown. Hatchling shell may be uniformly yellowish, reddish or olive-brown, or the areolae may be deep brown surrounded by a yellow border. Males easily distinguished by their faded patterning, plastral concavity, very large tail, and larger tail spine than females.

Subspecies Two, sometimes three, subspecies recognised. The typical race (*K. b. belliana*) is restricted to the east, and usually has 5 claws on each forefoot. The Western Hinged Tortoise (*K. b. nogueyi,* see pg 19) occurs in western Africa and has only 4 claws on each forefoot. There are also subtle differences in the relationship of plastron sutures between the two races, and it is likely that the two races should be treated as full species. The population on Madagascar is also sometimes treated as a separate race (*K. b. domerguei*), but this status seems undeserved as it appears to have been introduced by man.

Habitat In the east, wet savannah, coastal grasslands and dune forest edge. In the west, the edges of humid forest and isolated moister habitats in the Sahel region.

Distribution The most widespread of the Hinged tortoises, found in two disjunct populations either side of the rainforest of the Congo Basin. The typical race occurs from Somalia south to KwaZulu-Natal and west into the DRC, and has been introduced on Madagascar. The western African race extends from Senegal and the Gambia to Cameroon.

Biology Prefers humid microhabitats, and aestivates during dry periods, either in animal burrows or under dead logs. Omnivorous, feeding on fallen fruits, fungi, grasses, sedges and insects. In some areas it prefers millipedes, in others snails, which it eats after breaking the shells. Even known to eat sugar cane. When captured some specimens struggle, and may empty their bowels before retreating into their shells and closing the hinge. Breeding poorly known; nesting occurs throughout summer (November–April) in the south, and the female may lay a number of clutches (at 40-day intervals) of 2–7 (sometimes 10) elongate eggs (39–48 x 32–36 mm, 23–32 g). Incubation takes 90–110 days; hatchlings (38–40 mm) have been found in September–October and March–April. In West Africa nesting may occur in May, and clutches are smaller, comprising 2–4 oval to elongate eggs (28–38 x 41–45 mm). It has lived for up to 22 years in captivity.

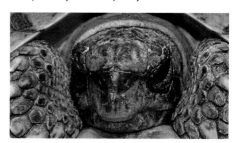

ABOVE AND TOP: Head of adult Bell's Hinged Tortoise showing the uncuspid beak.

ABOVE: Miombo woodland in Niassa Game Reserve.
LEFT: Adult Bell's Hinged Tortoise.

CONSERVATION Not formally threatened, but should be monitored. Although large numbers were once exported for the international pet trade from Ghana, Togo, Tanzania and Mozambique, this trade has declined in recent years. However, both the western and eastern populations are still in decline due to habitat loss. Frequent fires in the eastern savannahs also kill many tortoises, as well as altering habitat structure and food availability.

Speke's Hinged Tortoise
Kinixys spekii   Gray 1863

Other common name: **Savannah Hingeback**

Named after Captain John Hanning Speke (1827–1864), English explorer and discoverer of the source of the Nile.

Description A medium-sized tortoise. Carapace smooth, elongate and flattened (to 200 mm), with smooth marginals and a well developed hinge. Nuchal narrow and elongate; vertebrals broader than they are long; supracaudal undivided, with a smooth underside. Plastron large, with slightly projecting gulars, a shallow anal notch, 2 moderately sized axillaries and a large inguinal. Head small, with a rounded snout, subdivided prefrontals and a large frontal. Beak has a single cusp. Front of each forelimb covered in large, overlapping scales, and with 5 claws. Males have a plastral concavity and longer, thicker tails. Juvenile carapace has a zonary pattern, each shield having a dark brown centre with concentric light and dark zones.

These may persist in males (which may also be uniform olive-brown to buff); in adult females, the dark zones break up into ragged rays. Plastron a uniform dirty yellow in males, with vague zonary pattern in females and juveniles. Colour usually fades with age, and old adults become uniform, smooth olive-brown or brown. The head is brown to tan or yellowish.
Habitat Savannah, coastal plain and dune forest, entering thornveld, often with rocky areas.
Distribution Savannahs of central and eastern Africa, through Zimbabwe to the northern provinces of South Africa, and along the Mozambique coastal plain as far south as Swaziland. To the west, extends through southern DRC and Zambia to western Angola.
Biology Active in the wet summer months,

aestivating underground during the dry season in rock crevices, old termite nests, animal burrows, or short burrows they make by scraping into earth embankments. Home ranges are large and they occur in low densities (2–3 per ha). Active for over 8 hours each day, perhaps because of lower food resources in savannah habitats. In the wet season in Zimbabwe, males move from grassland to wooded grassland and pure woodland, returning to grassland with the approach of the dry winter. This movement is less evident in females. Omnivorous, with a very varied diet that includes the leaves and flowers of small annuals, grass, mushrooms, *Syzygium* and other fruit. Invertebrates form an important part of their diet, particularly millipedes, which they attack by biting at or just behind the head. They eat giant land snails (*Achatina*) and may also chew old bones. In females, sexual maturity is reached in about 9 years (shell length 140 mm); males mature faster, at 7 years, and at a smaller size (120 mm). Adult females significantly larger than males, weighing nearly half as much again as males. Survival rates are low and over 80% of adult tortoises die from predation, attributed to mammals and ground hornbills. High mortality is offset by the rapid growth rate of juveniles. During the breeding season (September–November) males follow the path of females, possibly following scent trails. Females move out of their normal home range to lay their eggs, and choose nest sites in sandy, well drained soil, usually shaded by large trees. Egg laying takes place in the evening, which allows the female to assess whether the site is warm enough for egg development, and also to avoid heat stress whilst digging. Eggs are laid about 8 cm beneath the surface. Clutch size varies from 2–6, usually 3–4, and eggs measure 33–47 x 28–34 mm and weigh 19–31 g. Larger females lay big clutches, and more than 1 clutch may be laid in a season. Hatchlings have 30–50 mm carapaces and are found from November to April.

Plastron (top) and carapace (above) of Speke's Hinged Tortoise.

CONSERVATION Not considered threatened, due to their wide range. Not harvested significantly for the pet trade, and few are targeted for human consumption. Recorded from numerous protected reserves, including the Kruger National Park. Some populations are probably in decline due to increased fire risk associated with human agriculture in savannah habitats.

Adult Speke's Hinged Tortoise.

Rocky thornveld near the Limpopo River, South Africa.

Lobatse Hinged Tortoise
Kinixys lobatsiana   Power 1927

Other common name: **Lobatse Hinge-back Tortoise**

Named after the Lobatse region, eastern Botswana, from where the first specimens were collected.

Description A medium-sized Hinged tortoise (females to 200 mm) with an elongated, rather narrow carapace. Nuchal narrow and elongated. Vertebrals with a shallow, central keel, broader than they are long. Supracaudal scute undivided, with a longitudinal groove on the underside. Rear marginals serrated and slightly upturned. Hinge well developed. Plastron large. Gular scutes protrude only slightly, and may lack a medial notch, and the anal notch is shallow. 2–3 small axillaries, and a moderate to large inguinal. Plastral concavity well developed in mature males. Snout does not project. Upper jaw only slightly hooked and unicuspid. Prefrontals subdivided; large frontal scale usually undivided. Each forelimb covered at the front in large, overlapping scales, and with 5 claws. Juveniles and females have a broken radiate pattern on each carapace shield, and each shield has a red-brown centre. Males usually uniform brown. Plastron uniform dirty yellow in adult males, but with sparse, dark, radiating streaks in females and juveniles. South African populations are more distinctly marked than those from Botswana.

Habitat Inhabits rocky hillsides with mixed *Acacia* and *Combretum* woodland to tropical bushveld, thornveld and *Burkea* savannah.

Distribution Northern South Africa and southeastern Botswana.

Biology The most arid-adapted Hinged tortoise, most active after summer rains; aestivates in burrows and rocky retreats during the cold, dry season. Diet varied, and includes mainly annuals, grass and fruit, but also mushrooms, beetles, snails and millipedes. A female is known to have laid 6 large eggs (30 x 40 mm) in mid-April. Hatching occurred after 313 days, a protracted incubation that was probably extended by a winter diapause.

CONSERVATION Range restricted, but large parts fall in protected areas, including private ecotourism and hunting concessions. Not considered threatened.

Adult Lobatse Hinged Tortoise.

The Lobatse Hinged Tortoise has a unicuspid beak.

Natal Hinged Tortoise
Kinixys natalensis   Hewitt 1935

Other common name: **Natal Hinge-back Tortoise**

Named after the South African province of Natal (now KwaZulu-Natal), from where the first specimens were collected.

Description Small Hinged tortoise (female shell length to 160 mm, 650 g; male shell length to 130 mm, 300 g). Carapace elongated, slightly domed, with a flat dorsal surface and sloping sides; hinge poorly developed. Nuchal elongate, all vertebrals broader than they are long, supracaudal usually divided. Paired gulars jutting only slightly beyond the carapace rim, more than twice as wide as they are long, and unnotched or weakly notched. 12–13 marginals on each side, smooth at the front, but slightly serrated at the rear. 2–3 axillaries. Head with a hooked, tricuspid beak (see p.13); prefrontal divided lengthwise; large frontal undivided; other head scales small and irregular. Each forefoot with 5 claws, and covered at the front with large, overlapping,

sometimes pointed scales. Buttock tubercles absent. Tail has a terminal spine, which is large in males. Males lack a concave plastron and are smaller than females. Carapace scutes have concentric patterning, with the light centres surrounded by concentric rings of orange-yellow and black-brown. Plastron has a similar ringed pattern, although this may be faded in adults. Head, limbs and tail brown to yellow.

Habitat Dry rocky thornveld and bushveld at 300–1 000 m elevation; mesic thicket in the south.

Distribution Mainly endemic to South Africa, from KwaZulu-Natal lowlands, through the Lebombo Mountains between Swaziland and Mozambique, to the lowveld of Mpumalanga.

Biology The most poorly known tortoise in South Africa, and the smallest Hinged tortoise. Hibernates during the winter dry season (May–September). Omnivorous, like other Hinged tortoises; eats insects in addition to small annual plants. In captivity copulation observed in February, and small clutches of 2 eggs laid in April, hatching in September after 5–6 months incubation. Hatchlings are large (35 mm in length, weighing 8–10 g).

CONSERVATION Previously considered Near Threatened due to its restricted range. However, it is recorded from major protected areas, such as Kruger National Park in the north and Weenen Nature Reserve in the south. Only small numbers may be harvested for tribal medicine. The main threat is from agricultural development that results in habitat loss and small, fragmented populations.

ABOVE: Adult Natal Hinged Tortoise.
ABOVE LEFT: Kruger Park bushveld is a typical habitat.

Pancake Tortoise

Malacochersus   Lindholm 1929

The genus name derives from its light and flexible shell (Greek; *malaco* = soft, *chelone* = a tortoise).

   Due to their unique, extremely flattened, soft shells, these tortoises have always been included in a genus on their own.

Pancake Tortoise

Malacochersus tornieri   (Siebenrock 1903)

Other common names: **Crevice Tortoise, Soft-shell Tortoise, Tornier's Tortoise**
Named in honour of the German taxonomist Gustav Tornier.

Description A smallish tortoise (females to 180 mm, males to 167 mm). Easily recognised by its extremely flattened shell, although hatchling shell is slightly domed. Shell very light and flexible, as the underlying bone retains the juvenile gaps. Marginals (11–12 on each side) shallowly serrated and slightly upturned at the rear. Supracaudal usually divided; nuchal long and narrow. Plastron with paired gular scutes, much broader than they are long. 2–3 small axillary scutes and 2–4 inguinals. Forelimbs at the front covered with large, overlapping scales; toes with 5 strong claws. Head moderate-sized; snout non-protruding; upper jaw hooked, and may be bicispid or tricuspid. Shell colour variable. Carapace yellow to tan, with light areolae on the centre scutes, with darker scute borders. Many individuals have a geometric pattern, with fine, radiating yellow stripes crossing the dark borders. Plastron yellow, with large brown blotches or jagged brown radiations. Head, limbs and tail yellow-brown. Hatchling shells light tan, with extensive irregular dark edges to the scutes. Males have longer tails, and relatively longer plastrons and narrower shells than the females.

Habitat Flat rocks and rocky outcrops (usually exfoliating granite) on low hills in savannah and woodland, at altitudes up to 1 800 m.

Head of adult Pancake Tortoise.

Adult Pancake Tortoise.

Pancake Tortoise retreating to a rock crack.

Distribution East Africa, from southern Kenya (Samburu District) to northern and central Tanzania, particularly in the Tanrangire region, with a recently discovered and isolated population in extreme northern Zambia. No records from Mozambique, despite the attempted trade of (probably smuggled) Pancake Tortoises from the region.

Biology Their very light shells allow the tortoises to crawl into narrow crevices or under rocks. Agile climbers, but do not forage far from their retreats, in which they aestivate during the dry season, preferring deep crevices in rock, in either horizontal or vertical positions. Active only 1 day in 4, they often remain inactive in their crevices. Most movement (50%) is made between crevices on the same rock outcrop, but nevertheless considerable movement does occur between rock outcrops, with males moving more frequently than females, possibly in search of mates. Juveniles rarely move between rock outcrops until they reach sexual maturity. Most activity occurs during the cool of the morning or late afternoon. Mainly herbivorous, eating grasses and succulents, but also gnawing on animal carcasses. Competition for mates is hard and males fight vigorously. In captivity sexual maturity is reached at 117 mm in males, 124 mm in females. Although male and females often share the same rock crevice, this seems a temporary arrangement and no extended pair-bond is formed. Courtship is aggressive, the male biting the limbs of the female as he trails her prior to mounting. Mating occurs in January–February; eggs are laid in July–August. A nest cavity is dug in loose sandy soil, and a single, elongate egg (37–50 x 22–39 mm, 11–13 g) is usually laid (rarely 2). 2 or 3 clutches are laid at about 40–45 day intervals. Hatchlings (37–40 mm, 7 g) emerge in December. Growth is rapid and sexual maturity may be attained in only 8 years.

CONSERVATION *2007 IUCN Red List* status Vulnerable. Once very popular in the international pet trade (1980s–1990s), due to their unique body form. Unsustainable collecting and damage to the habitat, such as overturned rock slabs, led to protection of the species, and collecting is now prohibited.

Tent Tortoises

Psammobates Fitzinger 1835

These small, attractive tortoises usually have their carapace scutes raised into knobs, with beautiful, radiating light and dark bands giving a striking geometric pattern. The carapace is domed and is never hinged. A nuchal is present. The paired gulars are longer than they are broad. Buttock tubercles are present in some species. Males are much smaller than females. '*Psammobates*' means 'sand-loving' (Greek *psammos* = sand, *bates* = one that treads or haunts), which alludes to their home in the arid interior of southern Africa, to which they are endemic. At present three species are recognised. One of these is very varied, comes in a bewildering range of shapes and colours, and has at times been considered to consist of no fewer than six species with 22 races. Another species is endangered due to habitat destruction. A single fossil species, *Psammobates antiquorum* (Broadley 1997), distinguished by its flattened shell, is known from early Pleistocene cave deposits (1.6–2.0 Ma) found at Sterkfontein in South Africa.

Tent Tortoise

Psammobates tentorius   (Bell 1828)

Other common name: **African Tent Tortoise**

Named after the raised, conical, tent-like vertebral and costal scutes on the carapace (Latin *tentorium* = a tent).

Description A small tortoise, with females growing larger (to 150 mm) than males (to 100 mm). Shell shape varies geographically; carapace scutes may be conical and raised, or flattened (see Subspecies). Nuchal typically broader than it is long, often minute, but rarely absent. Usually 11 (sometimes 10 or 12) marginals (numbers 4–7 being broader than they are high). Plastron large and well developed, and has a shallow anterior notch with paired gulars that are longer than they are broad. Deep anal notch, 2–3 (rarely 1) axillaries and an inguinal. Head moderately small, with a slightly projecting snout, upper jaw hooked, and bicuspid or tricuspid. Prefrontal may be divided longitudinally; frontals subdivided; other head scales small. Each forelimb with 5 claws, and covered on the front with large, irregular, overlapping scales. At least 1 buttock tubercle (which may be reduced or absent in the western race); heel of the hind foot with spur-like scales. Tail lacks terminal spine. Males with a plastral concavity and longer tails. Head, neck and limbs greyish brown to yellowish or reddish brown to tan. There may be some dark pigment on the head; snout may be yellow. Shell colour varies geographically, although the carapace usually has geometric patterning.

Subspecies A highly variable species; numerous populations have been named on the basis of slight differences in colour pattern or shape. Currently only three subspecies considered valid, and even the status of these is problematic.

Adult Karoo Tent Tortoise.

Head of Verroux's Tent Tortoise.

The typical race, *P. tentorius tentorius*, the common Tent tortoise, is large, usually with 13 marginals; carapace scutes strongly raised into conical 'tents', with a well marked pattern of yellow to orange radiating stripes on a black background. Plastron with solid mahogany markings in the centre and a yellow to orange edge. Occurs in the southern Karoo, from Grahamstown to Matjiesfontein, and entering the Little Karoo, intergrading with the next race in central Karoo.

Verroux's Tent Tortoise, *P. t. verroxii*, has 12 or fewer marginals; carapace with smooth or faintly raised scutes; a drab colour, usually with dull orange stripes on a dark brown background. Plastron with diffuse or indistinct dark brown patterning. Occurs in the northern Karoo, intergrading with the next race in Bushmanland and southern Namibia.

Trimen's Tent Tortoise, *P. t. trimeni*, is the most attractive and smallest race, with 12 marginals; carapace with small 'tents', well marked with rich orange-yellow stripes (shading to red around the marginals) on a black background. Dark brown centre of the plastron broken by lighter patches. Occurs in Namaqualand and southern Namibia, intergrading with the previous race in the east. A population in the vicinity of Helmeringhausen and Mariental in southern Namibia has a low, smooth shell and is uniform brown above and

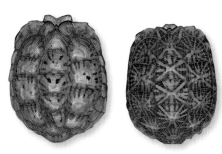

Shells of Verroux's Tent Tortoise.

below. Its taxonomic status remains unclear (the scientific name *bergeri* may be applicable).

Habitat Various habitats, including sandy desert, scrub karroid brush and succulent Karoo. Rainfall does not usually exceed 100 mm per year, except in the southeastern region.

Distribution Throughout the Great Karoo of South Africa, south to the northern slopes of the Suurberg near Grahamstown, and into the Little Karoo and adjacent valleys. In the west, found in the succulent Karoo, reaching the Cape west coast and north into southern Namibia.

Biology Not easily found, despite their wide range; often occur in low densities. Biology relatively poorly known. During droughts they burrow into sandy soil at the base of low shrub, emerging after the onset of rains. In the cooler parts of their range, they may hibernate from June to September, while others in warmer

Trimen's Tent Tortoise.

much of the year; only in winter (July–September) does egg formation cease. Eggs are first ovulated in October, and a single female may produce eggs over 3–8 months. Females retain the eggs for about 26–27 days before laying, although some clutches are retained for much longer. Most females breed each year and in good seasons, when food is plentiful, they produce either more small clutches of larger eggs, or more smaller eggs per clutch. This may be due to constraints placed on either egg size or egg number by the small volume of the female's body cavity. It is thought that the long breeding season of Tent tortoises is a response to the low and unpredictable rainfall occurring in their habitat. In the typical race, females produced small clutches of 1–3 eggs, and may lay from 1–6 (average 3.7) clutches between spring and late autumn. The smaller western races produce few eggs (1–2) and fewer clutches (1–4) per season. Eggs are almost ellipsoidal (27–34.5 x 21–24 mm) and hatch after about 220 days incubation. Eggs laid in autumn enter diapause and take longer to hatch. Hatchlings are about 25–33 mm long, weigh about 6–8 g, and are more circular in shape than adults.

parts of the range may aestivate in summer. Their geometric patterning provides very effective camouflage in broken shade at the base of bush. They drink by extending the rear legs and sipping the water that drains along the shell grooves to the forelimbs. They are active and feed in the cool of early morning and late afternoon. The diet includes grasses, such as *Stipagostris* sp., annuals, such as *Oxalis* sp. and *Gazania krebsian*, and small succulents, such as *Anacampseros* sp. Females of Verroux's Tent Tortoise, *P. t. verroxii*, in Namibia have home ranges of about 4 ha, and travel about 150 m each day whilst foraging for food. They rarely do well out of their natural range, and have lived for only 7–8 years in captivity. Enemies include small carnivores – rock monitors, eagles, goshawks, crows and even ostriches.

In the southern part of the range, where habitats are more mesic and the activity season longer, gravid females are found throughout

CONSERVATION Not currently considered threatened, due to their wide distribution. However, Trimen's Tent Tortoise is restricted to succulent Karoo and it is predicted that this habitat will be severely affected by ongoing climate change.

Succulent Karoo, such as seen here in the Richtersveld, is a typical habitat of Trimen's Tent Tortoise.

Geometric Tortoise

Psammobates geometricus (Linnaeus 1758)

Other common name: **Geometric Tent Tortoise**
Named after the radial geometric pattern that adorns the scutes.

Adult Geometric Tortoise showing its distinctive carapace.

Description A small tortoise; female shell averages 125 mm (to 165 mm) and weighs 436 g; males average 106 mm (to 123 mm) and weigh 207 g. Carapace very domed, with steep sides and a deep notch at the front with a small nuchal. Vertebrals broader than long, becoming raised and cone-like with age. 11–12 marginals: numbers 4–7 higher than they are broad, and those at the rear slightly upturned. Supracaudal not divided. Plastron large, with shallow anterior notch; paired gulars longer than they are broad. Single axillary and inguinal; deep anal notch. Males with an obvious plastral concavity. Head of moderate size; snout rounded; head scales small, except for a longitudinally divided prefrontal and subdivided frontal; upper jaw hooked. Forelimbs with 5 claws, and covered with small scales with scattered, larger scales. Buttock tubercles absent; tail lacks terminal spine. Carapace beautifully marked with geometric patterns; scutes with yellow centres from which yellow rays (8–15 on the vertebrals, 9–12 on the costals and 2–4 on the marginals) radiate, separated by black. Plastron yellow, with radiating faint black rays and bands. Limbs dark brown. Many juveniles with single yellow 'X' on each carapace scute and black plastron; the radial pattern develops with age.

Habitat Low-lying west coast renosterveld.

Distribution Endemic to the southwestern Cape, and now occurring in isolated populations around Ceres and Worcester, where it is restricted to small pockets of natural habitat. Largest population occurs in the Elandsberg Private Nature Reserve.

Biology Diet includes substantial amounts of geophytes (e.g. *Oxalis* spp. and *Pelargonium* spp.) and grasses (e.g. *Briza maxima, Cynodon dactylon Themeda triandra*); eat more than 27 different species of plants. Snails and the remains of young Parrot-beaked Tortoises have been found in faeces, probably eaten for their calcium content. Active in the early morning and afternoon, often in cold conditions. Enemies include crows and secretary birds, small carnivores and man; fires kill others. Probably live for longer than 30 years; sexual maturity attained in 7–8 years. Growth is relatively rapid, with 2 growth rings being laid down each year. Females are more common than males. A single clutch of 2–5 eggs (32 x 24 mm) is laid in spring (September–November) at the base of a grass tussock, usually on a north-facing slope. The eggs hatch in March–May, after 150–210 days of incubation, and hatchlings (30–40 mm, 7 g) emerge with first winter rains.

Juvenile Geometric Tortoise.

Elandsberg Private Nature Reserve in the Western Cape.

Serrated Tortoise

Psammobates oculifer   (Kuhl 1820)

Other common names: **Kalahari Tent Tortoise, African Serrated Star Tortoise**

Named after the radiating (Latin *oculus* = eye) pattern on the shell scutes.

Description A small tortoise, averaging 80–120 mm in shell length (females to 147 mm). Shell low and domed, with steep sides; shallow notch at the front, with a large nuchal, which may be divided. Scutes only slightly raised, with prominent growth rings. Vertebrals broader than they are long. Marginals (10–12, usually 11) strongly serrated at both the front and back. Plastron large and well developed, tapering to the front, with a shallow anterior notch; paired gulars wider than they are long. Single axillary and inguinal; deep anal notch. Head relatively small; snout rounded; upper jaw hooked, usually tricuspid. Prefrontals divided longitudinally and the frontal subdivided; other head scales small. Front of each forelimb with 5 claws, a few large scales, and 1 extremely large scale. Buttock tubercles present. Tail lacks a terminal spine.

Head of a Kalahari Tent Tortoise.

Males smaller than females, with a flatter shell, an obvious plastral concavity, a longer tail and a curved supracaudal. Carapace light brown-yellow, with each scute beautifully marked with a radial pattern of 6–10 dark brown to black rays. Plastron yellowish, with radiating dark rays. Head and neck tan to brown with some yellow markings. Jaws yellow. Limbs brown.

Habitat Arid savannah and scrub desert.

Distribution Endemic to southern Africa, from western South Africa (Limpopo, North West, Mpumalanga and Free State provinces), northwest through the Kalahari Desert of Botswana and Namibia. Do not occur south of Orange River, and have not been recorded from Angola (although they may occur).

Biology Poorly known, despite their wide distribution. During dry years, eat mainly succulents, and grasses if they are available (up to 38 plant species, with *Crotalaria sphaerocarpa* and *Nemesia fruticans* being most popular). Eat more annuals, herbs and grasses during the wet season, although the diet is less varied (17 species, most commonly *Tribulus terrestris*, *Aristida congesta* and *Indigofera alternus*). Also eat sheep and game droppings. During the cold, dry months (March to September) they lie dormant, often half buried in red sand at the base of a grass clump, or under fallen Acacia leaves and branches. Old mammal burrows may also be used as retreats. Females lay 1–2 eggs (28–31 x 40–42 mm) in December. They cannot swim, and permanent rivers (for instance, the Orange River) form barriers to dispersal.

> **CONSERVATION** Not considered threatened, due to their very large range, which has a low human density and little agricultural impact. Historically, the shell was used by Bushmen to make buchu pouches. Despite legal protection, they are still killed to be made into tourist goods, but the current level of exploitation appears sustainable.

Adult Kalahari Tent Tortoise.

Semi-desert scrub near Upington provides the ideal habitat for the Kalahari Tent Tortoise.

Tent Tortoise Shells

Shell colour, shape and pattern are very consistent in the Geometric and Kalahari Tent tortoises. In the other Tent tortoises, however, the shell variation is bewildering.

Geometric Tortoise

Serrated Tortoise

Tent Tortoise

Trimen's Tent Tortoise

Verroux's Tent Tortoise

Leopard Tortoise

Stigmochelys   Gray 1873

The genus name derives from Greek (*stigma* = mark, spot, *chelone* = tortoise).

   A monotypic genus related to the southern African radiation of small tortoises, including the Padlopers (*Homopus*), Tent tortoises (*Psammobates*) and Angulate tortoises (*Chersina*).

Leopard Tortoise

Stigmochelys pardalis   (Bell 1828)

Other common names: **Mountain Tortoise, Bergsklipad**
Named after the spotted shell (Greek *pardos* = leopard).

Description Maximum adult size varies geographically; larger in mesic habitats at the southern and northern extremes of the range. In the central savannahs of East Africa, reaches a maximum of 300–450 mm and a weight of nearly 13 kg. In the Eastern Cape, South Africa, and in the Ethiopian highlands and mesic areas in Somalia, adults average 15–20 kg and may exceptionally exceed 700 mm in length and 40 kg in weight. Hatchling carapace round, flattened and serrated. Adult carapace very domed, with steep sides, notched at the front but without a nuchal, and with slightly raised vertebral scutes (smooth in juveniles and very old adults). 10–12 marginals, with those on the rear edge usually serrated and often upturned. Vertebral 1 as long as or longer than it is broad, the others broader than they are long. Supracaudal undivided, usually down-turned. Plastron well developed, with paired gulars as long as they are wide, a deep anal notch, 2 axillary scutes (1 large, 1 minute), and a single inguinal. Head moderately large; snout non-protruding; upper jaw hooked,

Head of a Leopard Tortoise.

often tricuspid. Prefrontal large, may be single or divided longitudinally; frontal usually absent; other head scales small. Front of each forelimb with 5 claws, and covered with longitudinal rows of large, irregularly shaped, spiny scales. 2–3 buttock tubercles on each hind limb; tail lacks a terminal spine. Hatchling carapace yellow, with central paired or single black spots that may partially fuse. The ground colour becomes darker and more heavily blotched and streaked in black with age. Seams usually light-coloured and black smudges occur on the marginals. Old adults often uniform dark grey-brown. Head uniformly yellow or tan. Limbs and tail yellow to brown. Populations in drier habitats with lighter shells than those in wetter regions. Plastron yellowish, often with black radiating streaks and spots. Males with a longer tail than females, and a well developed plastral concavity. **Subspecies** Two races are sometimes recognised, although there remains controversy as to whether these races reflect definable populations linked to comparable genetic divergence. The typical race, *S. p. pardalis*, restricted to the eastern and southern Cape, with a relict population in southern Namibia, is defined by a larger plastral concavity in males, a larger adult size, and 2 spots on the vertebral scutes in hatchlings. The northern

Leopard Tortoise hatchlings.

race, *S. p. babcock*i, occurs throughout the rest of the vast range, and reaches a smaller size, with plastral concavity restricted to the rear of the plastron in males, a bolder coloration and only 1 spot on the vertebral scutes of hatchlings. However, extreme northern populations in mesic habitats in Ethiopia and neighbouring Sudan also grow very large and do not conform morphologically to the race *S. p. babcocki*. **Habitat** Varied, including karroid fynbos in the south, mesic thicket, arid and mesic savannah, thorn scrub, and grasslands, from sea level to over 2 900 m.

The Leopard Tortoise has a domed carapace with steep sides.

Distribution Throughout the savannahs of Africa, from southern Sudan, Ethiopia and Somalia, southward through East Africa to the Eastern Cape and Karoo, westward to southern Angola and Namibia. In arid areas, restricted to mesic habitats. Historically absent from the southwestern Cape and the former Transkei, adjacent KwaZulu-Natal, and Lesotho, but released captives found in many areas.

Biology Diet includes a wide variety of plants (over 70 documented species). Show seasonal preferences for food plants, selecting annuals such as *Hermannia quartiniana*, in South Africa, and *Tribulus terrestris*, in Namibia, followed by grasses such as *Eragrostis lemanniana*, and succulents such as crassulas and spekboom. Also gnaw bones, and even hyaena faeces, to obtain calcium for shell growth and eggshell development. May be active throughout the day, depending on temperature. In hot seasons, only a small proportion of tortoises are active each day; activity may occur in the early evening. To escape the heat of the day, they push into thick bush. Activity is greatly reduced during the dry season, although basking may occur. In many areas the dry season coincides with cool temperatures and so feeding also ceases.

Home range size varies considerably, depending on habitat use, seasonal activity and sex. The total range of an individual may be over 350 ha or as small as 18 ha, and usually contains

Leopard Tortoise.

much smaller core areas where 70% of activity is restricted. These cores are usually associated with available foods, although females may also undertake large movements associated with finding suitable egg-laying sites. Male home ranges are usually smaller (to 23 ha). Both sexes are known to undertake long return journeys (25–50 km) when translocated from their homes. Tortoise densities are very low (1.7 per 100 ha) in the semi-arid Nama Karoo habitat, compared with mesic thicket habitats in the Eastern Cape (up to 85 per 100 ha).

The hatchlings and juveniles have many predators, including rock monitors, storks, crows and small carnivores, whilst ants may attack the eggs. Adults are relatively immune to predation, except by man. Many adults have cracked shells from falls in rocky areas, while others are scarred

A Leopard Tortoise emerging from a rocky pool.

or killed in veld fires. They are usually well infested with ticks in the soft skin of the neck and upper limbs.

Growth in the first years of life is relatively slow, but increases rapidly as the young get too large to be killed by small carnivores, and can feed further from cover. They weigh about 1 kg by 7–8 years; thereafter body mass may double every 2–3 years. Females grow faster than males, and sexual maturity is probably reached in 15 years, by which time growth has slowed. May live in captivity for 30–75 years. In Zimbabwe and the Nama Karoo there is significant sexual size dimorphism, with females growing 1.7–2.1 times heavier than males. In the Eastern Cape the average difference in size between the sexes is smaller; very large individuals of both sexes occur. The sex ratio varies between populations: male and female numbers are equal in the Eastern Cape and Nama Karoo; in Zimbabwe and Tanzania, populations contain fewer females, with a greater male survival rate.

As with many tortoises, males are combative, particularly in the breeding season. Combat between opponents involves pushing, butting and sometimes overturning one another. Mating is similarly robust, the male trailing the female often for some distance and butting her into submission. Copulation is a noisy affair, often accompanied by much straining and 'asthmatic' wheezing by the male. The gravid female selects a sunny, well drained site and excavates a flask-shaped pit (up to 250 mm across and deep) with her hind feet; she urinates copiously to soften hard soil. She refills the hole and may tamp down the soil by lifting and dropping her shell regularly on the spot. Females lay 6–15 large, almost spherical, hard-shelled eggs (32–41 x 35–44 mm, similar in size and shape to ping pong balls). Reports

The Karoo semi-desert is a favoured habitat.

of exceptional numbers (up to 30 eggs) may be based on multiple clutches. 3–7 clutches of similar size are laid at monthly intervals during the breeding season. Large females lay more clutches, and incubation may take 8–15 months, depending on the temperature (in captivity, eggs incubated at 28°C hatch in 8 months). Clutches laid late in the season take longer to develop as the eggs may enter diapause during cold spells. During the long development, the ground may become very hard, and hatchlings may have to wait for days, even weeks, for rain to soften the soil, allowing them to burrow to freedom. Hatchlings weigh 23–50 g and measure 40–50 mm.

CONSERVATION Between 1987 and 1991, Leopard Tortoises accounted for 76% of the tortoises exported for the pet trade from Africa. Declines in some areas of East Africa have been attributed to unsustainable collecting for this trade. Populations in the Eastern Cape have also been affected by deaths on electric fences used to control the movement of problem mammals, such as warthog, porcupine and jackal. Overall, however, there is no evidence of range contractions or local extinctions; the species is not considered threatened.

Terrapins

Terrapins

Juvenile Okavango Hinged Terrapin.

Although terrapins, with 23 species, include the greatest diversity of African chelonians, they are not all closely related. The main group, with 18 species, comprises the side-necked terrapins – Pleurodira, the ancient chelonians that still withdraw their heads sideways beneath the carapace. In addition, there are five species of soft-shelled terrapins that draw their heads inward and belong to the more specialised Cryptodira.

A surprising absence

One of the surprises of African reptile fauna is the absence of a giant terrapin in the Congo Basin. The Congo River is Africa's largest river by far, and is famed for its giant fish, with the Goliath tigerfish, *Hydrocynus goliath*, growing to over 2 m. There is also the fabled *Mokele-mbembe*, a mythical dinosaur that has remained elusive (not surprisingly) despite numerous expeditions. In other continents, the major rivers are usually inhabited by at least one large – sometimes very large – freshwater chelonian. These include the Alligator Snapping Turtle, *Macrochelys temminckii*, from the Mississippi valley, the Amazon River Turtle, *Podocnemis expansa*, Bibron's Frog-faced Turtle, *Pelochelys bibroni*, from southern New Guinea, the Shanghai Soft-shell Turtle from China and Vietnam, the Indian Giant Soft-shell Turtle, *Chitra indica*, and the Black Soft-shell Turtle from the Brahmaputra River in Bangladesh. Sadly, many of these giants, which approach and often exceed a metre in shell length, are now endangered.

The largest African terrapin is the Nile Soft-shelled Terrapin, *Trionyx triunguis*, which is known from the coastal areas of the Congo River mouth, and a single, debatable record from above Kinshasa. It has not colonised the main drainage of the Congo River, as the waterfalls and rapids in the lower reaches of the river presumably block the terrapin's access. Chapin's Hinged Terrapin (which grows to 380 mm) is the largest species in the Congo River drainage. The largest hard-shelled African terrapin, the Serrated Hinged Terrapin, with a shell over 450 mm long, is also absent from the Congo Basin.

Okavango Hinged Terrapin.

Soft-shelled Terrapins
FAMILY TRIONYCHIDAE

These are unusual chelonians, whose scientific name refers not to their soft shells, but to the presence of only 3 claws on each foot. They are abundant in North America and southeast Asia, with only five African species in three genera. Fully aquatic, they come ashore only to lay their eggs, and occasionally to bask. The shell is flat and disc-like, with a flexible, cartilaginous edge. The horny shell is completely absent, and the body covered in leathery skin. The underlying bones that support the carapace are reduced with the loss of the peripheral bones. The plastral bones are even further reduced, and there are varied numbers of roughened areas, or callosities, overlying some of the plastral bony elements; these become larger with age. The neck is usually very long – often as long as the shell – and extendable, with a snorkel-like nose. Many grow to a large size. They are a shy, but active, omnivorous species. Active prey – fish, frogs and aquatic insects – are captured by gulp feeding (more correctly called hyoidal suction). The terrapin's long neck is shot forward toward the prey, whilst the large mouth explosively gulps open. At the same time the throat expands by movement of the hyoid bones, which creates a vacuum in the throat, and water rushes in, carrying with it the prey. In some species, for instance Aubrey's Flap-shelled Terrapin, the unusual flaps along the upper jaw restrict the inrush of water from the side, funnelling it through the front of the mouth. Large clutches of hard-shelled eggs are laid on land. All species are eaten by at least some people, depending upon their religious or cultural beliefs. None are critically threatened, although some populations are either overexploited, or have become locally extinct.

Three-clawed forelimb of Soft-shelled Terrapin.

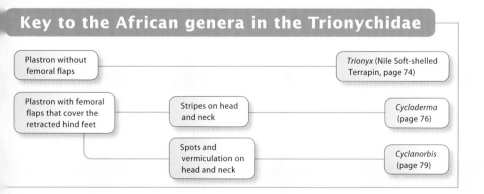

Key to the African genera in the Trionychidae

- Plastron without femoral flaps → *Trionyx* (Nile Soft-shelled Terrapin, page 74)
- Plastron with femoral flaps that cover the retracted hind feet
  - Stripes on head and neck → *Cycloderma* (page 76)
  - Spots and vermiculation on head and neck → *Cyclanorbis* (page 79)

Nile Soft-shelled Terrapin

Trionyx   Geoffroy Saint-Hilaire 1808

Previously contained many Asian and American Soft-shelled terrapins. Genus now contains a single living species, restricted to Africa and the Mediterranean region.

Nile Soft-shelled Terrapin
Trionyx triunguis   (Forsskål 1775)

Other common name: **African Soft-shelled Turtle**

Named because of the 3 claws on each foot (Latin *tri-* = three, *unguis* = nail, claw), from which the genus also derives its name (Greek *onyx* = nail, claw).

Description The largest African terrapin; females may reach 1 200 mm in length and over 60 kg. Males are smaller (to 65 cm). Plastron lacks flexible flaps over the hind limbs; head elongate and flattened, with a snorkel-like snout. Forelimbs have 3 sharp-edged, crescent-shaped skin folds. The young have indistinct median keels and wavy lines of tubercles on the carapace. These are lost with age, and the skin of adults is smooth. Carapace uniform olive to dark reddish brown in old adults, but usually with light-centred dark spots, often bordered with yellow, in juveniles. Plastron a uniform white to cream, but sometimes with a few light grey smudges. Head and limbs olive and heavily marked, with small yellow or whitish spots. Both chin and throat contain a network of large, white spots. Undersides of the limbs are yellow. Hatchlings greenish brown, with numerous dark-ringed, yellow spots. With age, the ground colour darkens and the light spots become smaller and more numerous.

Habitat Restricted to slow-moving rivers and streams, and enters flooded pans and oxbow lakes. Also found in estuaries and lagoons; large specimens enter coastal waters and the lower reaches of many Atlantic seaboard rivers.

Distribution Found in two main dispersed populations: the first in the east, in both the Blue and the White Nile (below Murchison Falls) drainages, including lakes Turkana and Albert, and extending downstream along the Nile into the eastern Mediterranean Sea as far as Turkey,

Estuarine habitat of Nile Soft-shelled Terrapin, Luango National Park, Gabon.

Dorsal (left) and ventral views of Nile Soft-shelled Terrapin.

Juvenile Nile Soft-shelled Terrapins are greenish brown; the colour darkens with age.

with isolated populations in the Jubba and Shabelle rivers, draining the Ethiopian highlands to Somalia; the second in the west, in most river drainages of West Africa, including the Niger River and Lake Chad, and south along the Atlantic drainage to the Cunene River mouth between Angola and Namibia.

Biology Active by day and night; capture prey by ambush when concealed in sand or underwater vegetation. Move fast in water and on land. Diet varied: adults eat mainly fish, tadpoles and adult amphibians (these items present in 61%, 53% and 35% respectively of the diet of specimens in Nigeria). Other prey includes aquatic and terrestrial crabs, insects and even small reptiles. May eat plants, such as palm nuts and dates; also scavenges on carcasses. Nesting usually occurs during the dry season, so as to avoid flooding of the nesting sites. Nests are dug in sand, earthen banks and on islands, and are about 15–20 cm in diameter and 20–25 cm deep. Several clutches may be produced per season. The white spherical eggs, about 32–39 mm in diameter, are hard-shelled, and clutches number around 30 (but up to 60). Incubation is rapid, and the eggs hatch in 76–78 days. The hatchlings are 42–54 mm long, and weigh 8–17 g. Females as small as 280 mm (3 kg) can reproduce; adults may live for over 50 years.

The very sharp and powerful jaws can inflict painful bites and may even amputate careless fingers.

Head of a Nile Soft-shelled Terrapin.

CONSERVATION Populations in sub-Saharan Africa readily exploited for food, but not considered immediately threatened. Exterminated or very rare in substantial parts of their former range, including the Egyptian Nile, Syria and Lebanon. Populations in coastal Nigeria have declined or become locally extinct following oil spillages. Mediterranean population Critically Endangered, with fewer than 1 000 adults remaining, and listed among the world's 24 most threatened chelonians by the Turtle Conservation Fund.

Flap-shelled Terrapins

SUBFAMILY CYCLANORBINAE

This small group of soft-shelled terrapins includes four African and two Asian species. The African species are divided equally into two genera that differ by the colour pattern on the head and neck, the relative thickness of the postorbital arch in the skull, and shape of the plastral bones.

When threatened, these terrapin initially try to flee into deeper water and burrow into soft sand or mud. If exposed on land they retreat into their soft shells, pulling in the head, tail and feet; the flexible edge of the carapace can deform over these regions. When the soft edge is retracted in this way it effectively closes the terrapins off from attack. Similarly, 2 semi-circular flaps close the holes in the plastron into which the hind feet are withdrawn. If the shell is seized, they can secrete an evil-smelling musk from special glands (Rathke's glands) next to the hind feet. If passive defence fails, they may bite and scratch powerfully, and try to run for water.

Striped Flap-shelled Terrapins

Cycloderma   Peters 1854

Endemic to Africa with two widely separated species.

Aubrey's Flap-shelled Terrapin

Cycloderma aubryi   (Dumeril 1856)

Other common name: **Aubry's Flap-shelled Turtle**

Named after Monsieur Aubry, a marine official who collected the original specimens.

Description A large terrapin (up to 610 mm and 18 kg); females grow larger than males. Oval carapace smooth in adults, but with a vertebral keel and numerous scattered tubercles in juveniles. Seven large and granulated plastral callosities cover most of the adult plastron. These are not as obvious in young terrapins. 5–8 enlarged, crescent-shaped scales on the anterior surface of each forefoot. Tail longer in males, and extends beyond the shell at maturity. Head elongate, with large eyes that look upward, elongate, snorkel-like snout, and lateral flange to the upper jaw that covers the lower jaw. Back red-brown in colour with a narrow, dark, vertebral stripe. Plastron yellowish, usually with brown stippling over the callosities, which may become extensive in some adults. Head brownish, with 5 thin stripes, the middle one extending backward from the crown to the neck. Upper lateral stripe extends from between the orbits to the back of the head. Lower lateral stripe begins at the nostril and extends backward through the eye to the neck. Chin and throat yellow, speckled with brown. Limbs brown. Hatchlings orange-reddish, with scattered black and white spots and a narrow brown vertebral stripe. Limbs almost black. Plastron orange-yellow, with prominent black blotches over the callosities. Thin black line extending from the snout, through the eye, and along the neck. The juvenile colour pattern becomes darker and more mottled with age.

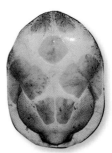

LEFT: Plastron, showing callosities and flaps to cover hind limbs.

BELOW: An adult Aubrey's Flap-shelled Terrapin.

Habitat Swamps, marshes and river pools in tropical rainforest. Leave the main rivers during the rainy season to hunt in pools in the flooded forest.

Distribution Congo rainforest, including Central African Republic, Gabon, Cabinda, Congo-Brazzaville and the DRC.

Biology Shelter among debris or shuffle into the sandy bottom, waiting in ambush for passing prey. Feed mostly at night; rarely seen except when basking on forest logs. Crabs, shrimps and fish form the main diet. Sexual maturity occurs at a carapace length of 30–32 cm. Egg laying occurs during the short dry season (January to March in Gabon); clutches of 15–35 almost spherical, hard-shelled eggs (30 x 39 mm, 17–22 g) are laid in shallow nests. A minimum of 2 clutches laid each season. Hatchlings, which measure up to 55 mm, appear in the main wet season (March–April).

The large Forest Water Monitor (*Varanus ornatus*) is a major predator of both eggs and hatchlings.

CONSERVATION Hunted for their meat and threatened with overexploitation in some regions, such as Gabon.

Flooded forest streams, such as this one near Rabi, Gabon, are favoured habitats of Aubrey's Flap-shelled Terrrapin.

Zambezi Flap-shelled Terrapin

Cycloderma frenatum Peters 1854

Other common name: **Zambezi Soft-shelled Turtle**

Named after the stripes on the side of the head and neck
(Latin *frenum* = bridle, rein).

The Zambezi Flap-shelled Terrapin has a pig-like snout.

Description A large terrapin (up to 560
mm and 14 kg). Carapace smooth in adults,
but with a vertebral keel and numerous
wavy longitudinal rows of small tubercles in
juveniles. Plastron has flexible flaps that cover
the hind limbs. Head elongate and flattened,
with a snorkel-like snout. Forefeet have 4 or
5 crescent-shaped skin flaps. The first claw
on the forefoot is usually enlarged. Adult
carapace uniform pale to dark olive, usually
with dark blotches. Juveniles may have a white
edge to the shell. Plastron white to flesh pink,
sometimes with grey infusions in adults. Head
and neck of the young grey-green, with broad

white stripes; these fade gradually in adult
specimens, in which the head and neck are
dark olive.

Habitat Inhabits clear streams, rivers and
lakes, preferring sandy bottoms.

Distribution Found in isolated drainages
from the Rufiji River drainage, Tanzania, south
to the Save River in southern Mozambique, just
reaching inland to southeastern Zimbabwe.
Also found in southern Lake Malawi and the
southern end of Lake Tanzania. Pleistocene
and Pliocene fossils are known from Lake
Turkana in northern Kenya, and from the
north end of Lake Malawi.

Biology Shy terrapins that rarely bask,
although they can be seen foraging in clear
water and often bask in warm surface waters.
Dig with their forelegs in soft mud for snails
and freshwater mussels, which are crushed
with their strong jaws. Enlarged first claw
on the forefoot probably used to excavate
molluscs, and is consequently often worn and
flattened. Fish, frogs and aquatic insects are
seized from ambush, when the terrapins are
concealed among the bottom debris. When
disturbed, they swim quickly into deeper

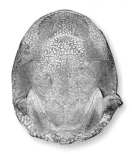

Plastron, showing callosities and the
flaps that cover the hind limbs.

Zambezi Flap-shelled Terrapin, showing its blotched shell pattern.

water, where they shuffle down, concealing themselves by scattering soft sediment onto their shells. Females come ashore at night on sandy beaches to lay eggs. A clutch of 15–25 hard-shelled, almost spherical eggs (30–35 mm) is laid in a 10-week period (January–April). Incubation is long (8–11 months); hatchlings (40–48 mm) emerge from nesting banks during the following rainy season. Predators include crocodiles and otters.

CONSERVATION Not currently threatened, although in some regions, such as Lake Malawi, local people eat the meat and eggs, and populations are consequently in decline. The meat is considered taboo by many people in coastal regions of Mozambique. Breeding females, emerging at night to lay eggs, are collected for food in Lake Malawi.

Lugenda River in Niassa Game Reserve, northern Mozambique.

Spotted Flap-shelled Terrapins

Cyclanorbis   Gray 1854

Endemic to Africa with two species restricted to West Africa and the Sahel region.

Nubian Flap-shelled Terrapin

Cyclanorbis elegans   (Gray 1869)

Other common name: **Nubian Soft-shelled Turtle**

Named after the brightly patterned (elegant) shell of the juvenile.

Description A large species (females up to 600 mm) with a rounded shell. Juvenile has rows of small tubercles and a low vertebral keel. Shell becomes smoother in adults, except for a series of enlarged tubercles rimming the neck. All dorsal bones are covered with small granulations. Callosities, which are absent in juveniles, develop with age. Adults have 4 plastral callosities, 2 large crescent-shaped ones at the front and 2 smaller ones to the rear. No gular callosities. Head relatively small, with a short bony snout with wide nostrils at the tip. 4 transverse, crescent-shaped skin folds on the front of each forefoot. Carapace olive to brown in adults with numerous yellow or light greenish spots on the lateral edges. Plastron yellow with dark spots. Head, in adults, brown with a light green or yellow vermiculation. Neck also brownish, but lighter in colour, with numerous small yellow spots; limbs brown. Hatchlings brightly coloured, with a green carapace, covered with large, irregularly shaped yellow spots, and a green to brown head with numerous yellow spots.

Habitat Slow-moving rivers, backwaters and marshes.

Distribution Isolated populations from the Sudan westward to Ghana.

Biology Due to its restricted and isolated distribution, one of the most poorly known African terrapin species; biology presumed to be similar to that of the Senegal Flap-shelled Terrapin.

CONSERVATION Range fragmented, due to encroaching desert in Sahel region, as growing human numbers and livestock increase pressure on remaining water bodies and threaten the survival of this rare terrapin. Near threatened in 2007 *IUCN Red List of Threatened Species*; current status uncertain.

Senegal Flap-shelled Terrapin
Cyclanorbis senegalensis (Duméril and Bibron 1835)

Named after Senegal, from where the first specimens were obtained.

Description A large terrapin (up to 500 mm), with females growing larger than males. Carapace oval (rounder in juveniles) and somewhat domed, with enlarged tubercles on the anterior rim. Carapace smooth in adults, but with numerous wavy rows of tubercles and a low vertebral keel in juveniles. 7–9 well developed plastral callosities, which are absent in juveniles, develop with age. Additional small callosities may occur in the gular region. Head moderate in size with a short, bony snout. 5 or 6 transverse, crescent-shaped skin folds on the front of each forefoot. Carapace brown to dark olive grey above, often mottled, with dark spots and a light border. Plastron white to cream, with extensive grey spots and blotches. Callosities may become green. Hatchlings have grey-brown carapace with scattered black vermiculation and irregular yellowish spots. Head finely spotted with yellow, throat and chin yellow-white. Head, with age, becomes olive to brown above, lighter laterally, and with darker

Juvenile Senegal Flap-shelled Terrapin.

Typical West African riverine bush habitat of the Senegal Flap-shelled Terrapin.

mottling on the chin and throat. Neck and limbs olive to grey-brown.

Habitat Rivers, streams, and lakes in gallery forest, extending into savannah marshes and ponds in the rainy season.

Distribution From Sudan, westward through Cameroon to Senegal, and south to Gabon.

Biology A shy, elusive species that rarely basks. Up to 12 eggs (25 x 45 mm) are laid in March–April in shallow nests that may be some distance from water. Several clutches of eggs may be laid each season. Diet varied, including fallen fruit and small aquatic animals. May also pick flesh from dead carcasses.

> **CONSERVATION** Near threatened species, but they remain common in many areas. Readily eaten; often caught on hook and line in some areas. (*2007 IUCN Red List of Threatened Species.*)

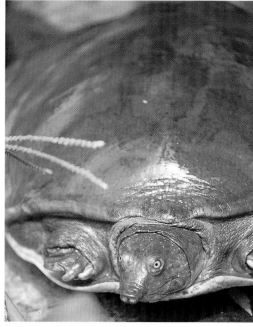
Adult Senegal Flap-shelled Terrapin.

Side-necked Terrapins
SUBORDER PLEURODIRA

Globally, side-necked terrapins have a curious distribution, being restricted to the southern continents of South America, Africa, Madagascar and Australia. These form an ancient lineage; their common ancestor lived on the ancient megacontinent of Gondwana. Australian and most South American side-necked terrapins are placed in the family Chelidae. The remaining South American side-necks, along with a single species from Madagascar, are included in the Podocnemididae.

FAMILY PELOMEDUSIDAE

The African genera *Pelomedusa* and *Pelusios* are closely related, and are placed together in the Family Pelomedusidae. The most obvious feature of the group is that the neck can be completely retracted sideways under the carapace edge – hence their common name. The carapace lacks nuchal and supracaudal scutes, whilst the plastron has an intergular scute. In all species the nostrils are set at the end of the snout to allow for breathing at the surface. The forelimbs have strong claws, used for shredding food. They swim with alternate strokes, mainly of the hind limbs, which have webbed edges. Small tentacles beneath the chin appear to be used in mating. Reproduction is similar in all species: the females emerge on land to dig nest holes with their hind feet in soft, moist soil above the flood mark. If the ground is hard, they urinate to soften it. The eggs, like those of sea turtles, but unlike those of other African chelonians, are soft-shelled.

A Marsh Terrapin hatching from its soft-shelled egg.

A young Marsh Terrapin.

Key to the African genera in the Pelomedusidae

Plastron not hinged at front ———————————— *Pelomedusa* (Marsh terrapins)

Plastron hinged at front ———————————— *Pelusios* (Hinged terrapins, p85)

Marsh Terrapin
Pelomedusa Wagler 1830

The genus *Pelomedusa* contains a single species, widely distributed in sub-Saharan Africa, and also found on Madagascar, where it is probably introduced.

Marsh Terrapin
Pelomedusa subrufa (Lacepède 1788)

Other common names: **Helmeted Terrapin, Cape Water Terrapin**
Named after the plastron colour (Latin *sub* = below, *rufa* = reddish), which in fact is only reddish in some populations.

Description A largish terrapin (up to 325 mm); males may grow larger than females. Shell very flat, thin-shelled and lacks a plastral hinge. Head large, with 2 small tentacles beneath the chin, and musk glands on marginals 4–8 near the carapace edge. Hind feet with a webbed fringe. Males have longer tails and narrower, flatter shells than females. Shell uniform olive to dark brown above, sometimes with a black-edged shield and paler marginals. Plastron either entirely black, pale-coloured or with a symmetrical, pale-centred pattern, that may have a reddish edge. Head dark on top, with pale vermiculation, paler below and on the jaws.
Subspecies Two races are usually recognised: the northern race, *P. s. olivacea*, with olive colour and widely separated pectoral scutes, and the typical race, *P. s. subrufa*, found throughout most of the range, in which the pectorals are in contact.
Habitat Slow-moving and still water, particularly temporary wetlands.

Basking adult Marsh Terrapin.

Distribution The most widely distributed chelonians in Africa, found throughout sub-Saharan Africa and even on Madagascar. Only absent in extreme desert, closed-canopy forest and high montane grasslands.

Biology Locally common, even in semi-arid areas. Prefer shallow, temporary water bodies, even without aquatic vegetation. Usually absent from permanent water inhabited by crocodiles, as their thin shells offer little protection. May bask on land or on emergent rocks or logs, or by floating at the surface of the water. Bask out of water only when water temperatures are too low for warming. Not active at temperatures below 17°C. Aestivate during droughts by burrowing into moist soil, often far from their aquatic home.

Omnivorous, eating almost anything, including water weed, insects and frogs, with a higher proportion of plants than in the diet of Hinged terrapins. In some regions, such as Namibia's Etosha Pan and Tanzania's Serengeti, they behave like crocodiles and ambush, drown and devour doves and sand grouse that come to drink at shallow pans.

Many are killed on roads while migrating to new areas after good rains. They can live for over 16 years in captivity. Few people eat them, as they have an unpleasant, musky smell.

Mating occurs in water and the breeding season is extended. Usually 10–30 (but up to, and sometimes exceeding, 40) soft-shelled, elongate eggs (30–40 x 18–28 mm, 10 g) are laid in a flask-shaped pit. Young hatch at between 90 and 110 days, emerging after ground has been softened by rain. Hatchlings measure 25–38 mm and weigh 8–10 g.

> **CONSERVATION** The most widely distributed terrapins; rarely eaten and not threatened. Range in eastern and southern Africa has probably increased with the proliferation of farm dams and water points. Some populations in coastal Nigeria have become locally extinct following oil spillages.

Juvenile Marsh Terrapin; the dorsal keel disappears with age.

Marsh terrapins favour temporary muddy pans formed after rain, such as this one in South Africa's Karoo.

African Hinged Terrapins

Pelusios Wagler 1830

This is the most diverse genus of African terrapins, with at least 17 species. They have a range of common names, including mud turtles, forest turtles, side-necked terrapins and others. The scientific name derives from the Greek *pelos*, meaning mud or clay, which describes the wallows and puddles in which many species live.

They are distinguished by a prominent hinge in the plastron, from which the common name derives. The hinge runs along the pectoral-abdominal suture, and between the underlying hypoplastral and mesoplastral bones. It is closed by a large muscle that attaches to the axillary buttress. This hinge is pliable even in hatchlings, and allows the front of the plastron to close, protecting the head and forelimbs.

The large species often inhabit deep, open water in permanent lakes or large rivers, and have thick, heavy shells that help to protect them from crocodiles. The smaller species prefer muddy backwaters, shallow pans or flooded forest that fill with water only in the rainy season. When droughts come they may shuffle down into mud and enter a short aestivation, or migrate to more permanent water bodies. Mating occurs in water, and is possible only if the female is willing. Clutches of soft-shelled eggs (5–50, depending upon the species) are laid in nests on sandbanks or in other suitable spots.

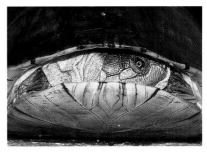

A number of Miocene and Lower Pleistocene fossils are known, of both living species, such as the Serrated Hinged Terrapin, and extinct species, such as *P. rusingae*, from Rusinga Island in Lake Victoria. The Seychelles Hinged Terrapin (*P. seychellensis*) became extinct c. 1950.

TOP TO BOTTOM: This sequence of photographs depicts the opening of the plastron hinge in the Hinged terrapin.

Adanson's Hinged Terrapin
Pelusios adansonii (Schweigger 1812)

Other common name: **Adanson's Mud Turtle**

Named after Michel Adanson, a French botanist who found the first specimens while exploring Senegal (1748–52), and after whom the Baobab tree (*Adansonia digitata*) is also named.

Description A small species that reaches a maximum shell length of 220 mm. Shell fairly deep, and broadest at the level of the hind limbs. Low keel down the centre of the backbone. Vertebrals at least as long as they are broad, or slightly longer; 4th vertebral the smallest, with rear margin smooth and rounded. Plastron with long, rounded anterior lobe; plastral hinge does not fully close. Posterior lobe narrow and ridged, with a well developed anal notch. Axillary or inguinal scutes absent. Head broad, with the snout slightly projecting. Upper jaw smooth, without a hook or notches. Frontal scale on the head very large, with 2 barbels beneath the chin. Feet well clawed, but with only a narrow fringe to aid swimming. Head grey-brown with yellow vermiculation above, yellowish on the sides and jaw. A yellow stripe may extend from the eye to the ear drum. Eye emerald green. Carapace blackish brown, lighter laterally, sometimes with darker radiations or spots, but with black marginals. Plastron black-edged, with a streaky yellowish centre, fading with age to a yellow ivory with black outer tips to some of the scutes. Skin of neck, tail and limbs yellow, with darker outer surfaces to the limbs.

Habitat Backwaters and pools in upper reaches of major rivers of the Sahel (White Nile, Niger, Senegal), including Lake Chad; absent from the smaller rivers draining the Atlantic rainforests.

Distribution Most northern species, found in scattered spots in the Sahel region, from the White Nile in Sudan, westward through Chad to Cameroon, Nigeria, Mali, Liberia, Senegal and Gambia.

Biology The lives of these small terrapins remain poorly known. Clutches containing up to 15 eggs (29.5–33 x 18–19 mm) may be laid up to 4 or 5 times in a season. Feed mainly on aquatic invertebrates, particularly molluscs. With the onset of the dry season, they burrow down into mud at the bottom of the pond, spending several months aestivating underground.

Adult Adanson's Hinged Terrapin.

Typical riverine habitat of Adanson's Hinged Terrapin.

CONSERVATION Although still locally common and widely distributed through the Sahel region, many are now eaten by rural people as more traditional food, such as fish and game, dwindle due to human population growth and the encroaching desert. In the face of global warming and human pressure, the surviving populations need to be monitored in case they become threatened.

Okavango Hinged Terrapin
Pelusios bechuanicus FitzSimons 1932

Other common name: **Okavango Mud Turtle**

Named after the British colonial Bechuanaland Protectorate (Botswana) in which the Okavango Delta occurs.

Description A large species (females to 330 mm, males smaller). Shell heavy, elongate and broader to the rear, where it has a smooth posterior edge. Backbone of juvenile shells raised into a prominent keel, but this almost disappears in large adults. Growth rings on the shell are shallow. Plastron with strong narrow hinge that closes tightly. Intergular large and elongate. Head very large and broad, with a blunt snout. Upper jaw with no cusps; 3 tentacles beneath the chin. Feet with strong claws; crescent-shaped scales on the front of the forelimbs only weakly developed. Head black, with symmetrical yellow markings, which are bolder in juveniles. Skin of the limbs, tail and neck grey-yellow. Carapace black and shiny, sometimes tinged with orange-yellow on the sides. Plastron black, sometimes yellowish in the centre, and often with white seams.

Habitat Prefer gentle, clear backwaters of rivers and swamps.

Distribution Centred around the Okavango Delta of northern Botswana and adjacent Namibia and Zimbabwe, extending along the Okavango River into eastern Angola and the Kafue Flats in Zambia.

Biology A poorly known, shy species, often seen swimming in the clear waters of the Okavango Delta. Large clutches (20–50) of elongate eggs (35–39 x 21–23 mm) are laid in moist soil in late spring (October in the Caprivi). Females are mature at a shell length of 239 mm. Fish and aquatic invertebrates form the main diet, and the Shoebill Stork, *Balaeniceps rex*, is a predator of young terrapins in the Kafue Flats.

ABOVE AND ABOVE LEFT: The Okavango Hinged Terrapin has a yellow-blotched head.

BOTTOM LEFT: Botswana's Okavango Delta.

CONSERVATION Range largely in protected areas (Moremi and Chobe game reserves in Botswana, and the Kafue National Park in Zambia). Not presently threatened, although many are caught in fish traps.

Turkana Hinged Terrapin
Pelusios broadleyi   Bour 1986

Other common name: **Broadley's Mud Turtle**

Named in honour of Don Broadley, Africa's foremost living herpetologist.

Description A small species (to 155 mm). Shell oval, broadest to the rear, with a prominent keel on all 5 vertebrals (which is more obvious in juveniles). Rear of the shell smooth and rounded. Anterior of plastron broad, with a large intergular. Plastral hinge weak, with little movement; the posterior part of the plastron narrows and has a deep anal notch. Femoral and anal scutes reduced. Axillary and inguinal scutes usually absent. Head broad, with a short, slightly projecting snout; upper jaw smooth.

Large transverse scales cover the anterior surfaces of the forelimbs, which bear long, strong claws. Carapace greyish brown, with many small, dark radiating lines on each scute. Plastron yellow in juveniles, with dark blotches towards the edge. These expand with age. Plastron in adults brown to black,

Narrow plastron of a Turkana Hinged Terrapin.

although an irregular yellow centre is usually present. Males have a well developed plastral concavity. Head brown, with light vermiculation above, and yellow upper jaws with dark spots or bars; chin and neck grey to yellow, with fine dark spots. Eye has a light emerald iris.

Habitat Shallow bays in Lake Turkana, and oases and seasonal streams in the area.

Distribution Known only from the shallow bays of Lake Turkana (also known as Lake Rudolph), Marsabit District, Kenya, and the adjacent streams and oases.

Biology Almost nothing is known of the lives of these small terrapins, due to the desolate, remote location to which they are restricted. May aestivate underground during dry periods. Prefer shallow water, and spend much of the heat of the day buried in shoreline sediments. Forage at night. Diet unknown, but probably includes invertebrates, particularly molluscs, and small fish. Nesting occurs at night, due to the extreme heat. Hatchlings are small, measuring only 25 mm.

> **CONSERVATION** Locally common, but with a very restricted range; considered Vulnerable (*2007 IUCN Red List*); eaten by local people.

This oasis near Loyangalani, Kenya, is a typical habitat of this species.

The head of Turkana Hinged Terrapin.

Keeled Hinged Terrapin

Pelusios carinatus   Laurent 1956

Other common name: **Keeled Mud Turtle**

Named after the prominent keel (Latin *carina* = ridge) along the top of the carapace.

Description A largish terrapin (up to 300 mm). Carapace elongate and oval, with a shallowly serrated, upturned rear margin. Vertebral keel well developed in juveniles, and persists in reduced form in adults. Plastron with rounded anterior lobe, short bridge, and narrow posterior lobe, ending in an anal notch. Axillary scute absent. Intergular about 1.5 times as long as it is broad. Males have a slight plastral concavity. Head largish and narrow, with a short snout, unnotched upper jaw, and 2 tentacles under the chin. A few enlarged transverse scales occur on the front of the forelimbs. Carapace uniform black. Plastron plain black or yellow, or with yellow blotch in the centre that leaves a black border, usually confined to the anterior lobe. Head brown or black, and reticulated with yellow in juveniles, often with a prominent yellow bar from the angle of the mouth to the tympanum, fading to yellow vermiculation in adults. Neck and limbs grey-yellow.

Habitat Inhabit thick mats of floating vegetation in oxbow lakes, backwaters and swamps in forest and adjacent savannah.

Distribution Restricted to the Congo River basin, from Gabon, Central African Republic and the DRC.

Biology A little-known species; during the rainy season may enter flooded savannah. Shy, and often active only in the later afternoon and early evening. Omnivorous, eating various water plants, including fallen forest fruits, insects, fish and aquatic shells. Females lay 6–12 eggs.

> **CONSERVATION** Still relatively abundant in the wild, although harvested with nets and fishing lines by local communities.

Head of an adult Keeled Hinged Terrapin.

Juvenile, showing pronounced keel along the back.

Adult Keeled Hinged Terrapin.

Western Hinged Terrapin
Pelusios castaneus (Schweigger 1812)

Other names: West African Mud Turtle
Named after the shell colour (Latin *castanea* = chestnut-coloured).

Description A medium-sized terrapin (to 285 mm). Carapace elongate and oval. Low, vertebral keel formed by a protuberance on the 4th vertebral. Vertebrals 2–4 as long as they are broad, or slightly longer. Shell widest at the level of the hind limbs; rear margin smooth. Plastron large, covering much of the lower carapace, with a short anterior lobe, and deeply notched posteriorly. Bridge broad, and lacks an axillary scute. Males have a slight plastral concavity.

Head largish, with a slightly protruding snout and 2 tooth-like cusps on upper jaw. 2 tentacles beneath the chin. Several enlarged transverse scales at the front of each forelimb. Carapace may be yellowish brown to olive, or dark brown to black. Plastron yellow, sometimes darker in the centre or along the outer edges of the sutures. Head olive brown, with faint, pale vermiculation. Neck and limbs greyish yellow. Hatchlings black with yellow blotches on the ventral side of the marginals and the plastron, and a yellow, interrupted stripe running from the eye to the ear on the dark grey head.

Plastron pattern.

Habitat Inhabit rivers, streams, marshes, swamps, lakes and shallow temporary ponds, preferring well shaded, permanent water bodies with moderate to dense vegetation.

Distribution Widely distributed in West Africa from Senegal to northwestern Angola, and inland to the Central African Republic. Also found on the island of São Tomé, and introduced to Guadeloupe in the Caribbean.

Biology Inhabit mainly temporary water bodies, and thus aestivate during dry spells, buried in moist mud. Omnivorous, and will eat fruits and plant material in addition to aquatic invertebrates (insects, molluscs and crabs). Small fish eaten by over 50% of these terrapins; gastropods and amphibian eggs more frequently eaten in the wet season. In Nigeria, home-range size similar for both females (2.6 ha ± 1.1 ha) and males (2.4 ha ± 1.5 ha).

During courtship, the male rhythmically bobs his head within the female's vision and tries to touch noses with her. Females prefer nesting sites with abundant vegetation and sandy soil, situated beside ponds, rather than on river banks. The breeding season is between February and March on the Ivory Coast. Clutch size varies from 6–27 soft-shelled elongate eggs (21–27 x 33–40 mm, 8–15 g).

Swamps, ponds and lakes are all favoured habitats.

Incubation takes 76–84 days (57–66 days in captivity). Hatchlings measure 35–44 mm in length and weigh 9–14 g. Females may be sexually mature with a shell only 131 mm long. Hatchlings shelter in thick bankside vegetation.

When captured they emit a foul-smelling oily yellow secretion from glands in the leg region.

> **CONSERVATION** Regularly harvested for food, and even stuffed and sold as tourist curios, yet wild populations of these wide-ranging terrapins not currently considered threatened. The species most resilient to oil pollution in Nigeria, although still in decline in the region (oil-polluted areas have 80% fewer terrapins than unpolluted areas).

Adult Western Hinged Terrapin.

Yellow-bellied Hinged Terrapin
Pelusios castanoides   Hewitt 1931

Other common name: **East African Yellow-bellied Mud Turtle**

Named because it looks similar to the previous species (Greek *eides* = like).

Description Medium-sized terrapin (up to 230 mm). Shell elongate and usually smooth. Low vertebral keel may be present on vertebrals 4 and 5; posterior marginals may be slightly serrated. Plastron with large, rounded anterior lobe with a strong hinge that closes the front opening. Posterior plastron lobe slightly constricted, with a deep anal notch. Bridge broad, but lacks an axillary scute. Head of moderate size, with a strongly bicuspid beak, and 2 tentacles beneath the chin. Several transverse rows of enlarged, crescent-shaped scales on the forelegs. Carapace olive, blackish brown or yellowish, and may have a marbled pattern of yellow and brown marks. Plastron yellow, usually with faint black markings on the front sutures. Head blackish brown, with fine yellow vermiculation. Skin of the neck and limbs is yellow-brown.

Subspecies Two races are recognised: the typical race, *P. c. castanoides*, occurs in Africa and Madagascar, replaced by *P. c. intergularis* in the Seychelles.

Yellow-bellied Hinged Terrapin.

Small swamps, like this one near Inhambane, Mozambique, are a preferred habitat of the Yellow-bellied Terrapin.

Habitat Prefer still lakes, backwaters and swamps at low altitude.

Distribution Found from coastal southern Kenya, south through the central Mozambique Plain to northern KwaZulu-Natal, South Africa, with isolated populations on Madagascar and the Seychelles.

Biology Frequent shallow water, burying themselves in mud when the water dries up, and re-emerging with the rains. Shells of many specimens are scarred from dry-season fires. Feed at night in summer, when water temperatures are high – in Lake Chilwa, Malawi, on aquatic insects and frogs, and particularly on large pulmonate snails and floating vegetation; in the Seychelles, on fruits, plant shoots, snails and crabs. Two females from Malawi were recorded laying 25 eggs (30–33 x 21–23 mm) each, at the end of September.

> **CONSERVATION** The typical race in Africa is not considered threatened, but the endemic race found on the Seychelles is considered Critically Endangered, as the population consists of only 300–350 individuals.

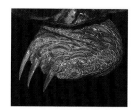

LEFT: A hind foot, showing long claws and lateral fringe.

BELOW LEFT: An adult scarred by fire.
BELOW: Adult Yellow-bellied Hinged Terrapin.

Central African Hinged Terrapin
Pelusios chapini Laurent 1965

Other common name: **Central African Mud Turtle**

Named in honour of James P. Chapin, an American explorer and ornithologist who, at the age of 19, and for 6 years (1909–1915), helped lead the American Museum Congo Expedition that collected natural history specimens in the region.

Description A large terrapin (carapace up to 380 mm). Shell narrow and flattened, with smooth marginals. Juveniles with a modest keel that is reduced or even absent in adults. Plastron large, with a deep anal notch; the hinge shuts tightly. Bridge broad, and lacks an axillary scute. Head with a slightly protruding snout; 2 cusps on the upper jaw.Carapace and plastron uniform black to dark brown; plastron may have yellowish or lighter brown medial patches. Brown head has irregular darker markings on the crown, but is lighter on the jaws. Feet strong, dark above, lighter below. Juvenile shell black with light radiating streaks.

Habitat Inhabit streams, rivers and lake margins along the rainforest edge and move into adjacent savannah in the rainy season.

Distribution Found in the northern Congo River drainage, from Uganda, through the Central African Republic, into the northern DRC and Gabon.

Biology An active species that moves in the rainy season from permanent water bodies into flooded savannah and temporary water bodies. Omnivorous, eating fallen fruit and plant material, in addition to fish, aquatic invertebrates, and even the carcasses of dead birds and mammals. Reproduction little known. In Gabon, a hatchling measuring 27 x 34 mm was recorded in February.

CONSERVATION Heavily exploited by local villagers, but not currently considered threatened.

ABOVE AND BELOW: Adult Central African Hinged Terrapin have a uniform black-brown carapace.

Streams at the forest edges are preferred habitats.

Forest Hinged Terrapin
Pelusios cupulatta   Bour & Maran 2003

Other common name: **Central African Mud Turtle**

Named after the wildlife centre, 'A Cupulatta' (Corsican for tortoise), which financed the expedition during which this new species was discovered.

Description A smallish terrapin (carapace up to 230 mm) with a round, flattish shell (height less than half its width). Juveniles with well developed vertebral keel, usually still visible in adults, particularly on the posterior vertebrals. Plastron large, closes completely, with a deep, narrow anal notch. Head wide and flattish, with a slightly pointed snout, an obviously hooked beak, and 2 tentacles beneath the chin. Numerous wide, rectangular scales cover the front of the forelimbs. Carapace uniform light or reddish brown, darkening with age, and with a dark, almost black median stripe along the vertebrals. Plastron usually of similar colour, sometimes darker; lower surface of the shell often bears a zigzag pattern around the edge that is composed of a paler triangular blotch on each marginal. Central sutures may also be cream coloured. Head dark brown

above, yellowish on the sides, with fine dark speckles. Iris of eye silvery grey. Juvenile colour pattern similar to that of other West African species, with a light brown carapace that has a black vertebral stripe. Marginals paler below, with dark sutures; costals have a dark smudge on the posterior centre. Plastron uniform dark brown.

Habitat Prefer small rainforest streams and swamps.

Distribution Presently known only from the Ivory Coast (Côte d'Ivoire), just extending into adjacent Liberia. Several old shells are reputed to have come from Nigeria, but the presence of the species in that country is unlikely, although they may occur in Ghana.

Biology Nothing is known about the lives of these small, recently described terrapins, which look like, and are found swimming together with, the Gabon Hinged Terrapin (see opposite), and probably have a similar biology.

> **CONSERVATION** Restricted distribution; discarded, broken shells around villages indicate that it is regularly eaten. Further research is required to determine whether it is threatened.

Juvenile Forest Hinged Terrapin shell.

Forest stream in Tai National Park, Ivory Coast.

Adult Forest Hinged Terrapin.

Gabon Hinged Terrapin

Pelusios gabonensis (Duméril 1856)

Other common names: **Gabon Mud Turtle, Central African Mud Turtle, African Forest Turtle**

Named after Gabon, from which the first specimens were obtained.

Description A large terrapin (up to 330 mm) with a flattened, rounded shell. Central keel along the vertebrals prominent even in adults, and very prominent in juveniles; rear of shell slightly serrated in juveniles, becoming smooth in adults. Large plastron, covering almost the entire opening, has a deep anal notch. Bridge not as rigid as in other species, being composed of cartilage. Plastron has a long anterior lobe and close-fitting hinge. Head broad, with a protruding snout that is rounded and not obviously hooked; upper jaw has a slight notch, flanked by 2 tooth-like cusps. 2 small tentacles beneath the chin. Anterior surfaces of the forelimbs covered in large, irregular scales, and strongly clawed, but have only a slight web.

Carapace buff to grey-yellow, with a distinct black vertebral stripe widening on the anterior marginals. Carapace darkens with age with black radiations to the scutes; very old, large individuals are almost totally black above and below, although plastron may have light yellow seams. Juvenile carapace light brown, with a prominent black vertebral stripe. Marginals paler below; plastron a uniform dark brown with paler seams. Head buff-coloured, with broad, black Y-shaped stripe connecting the orbits, and extending backward medially onto the neck. A second dark stripe may extend between the orbit and tympanum. Jaws and throat tan in adults, black in juveniles. Limbs of juveniles blackish, lightening to grey-yellow in adults.

Habitat Found in varied habitats, including marshes, swamps and flooded forest. In creeks and streams in tropical rainforest, they prefer acid water (pH 5.5–6.0). Large adults prefer the larger rivers.

Distribution Found in Liberia and Guinea in tropical West Africa, eastwards to western

Gabon Hinged Terrapin; juvenile (above) and adult (below).

Tanzania and through the Congo Basin and the Atlantic coastal region to northern Angola.

Biology About a dozen eggs (25 x 35 mm) are laid in a nest dug close to water. Hatchlings measure 42–43 mm, and after hatching move to quiet backwaters. Omnivorous, feeding on insects, worms, snails, and even fish. May also eat water plants and fallen fruit, and are often attracted to traps baited with fish.

> **CONSERVATION** Readily hunted for food throughout their range, but still relatively common and not currently threatened.

Maran's Hinged Terrapin
Pelusios marani   Bour 2000

Other common name: **Central African Mud Turtle**

Named after Jerome Maran, a young French naturalist who has travelled extensively in West Africa in search of chelonians, and who collected the first specimens of the Forest Hinged Terrapin (p 94).

Description A medium-sized terrapin (up to 275 mm) with an elongate shell. Keel along the backbone moderately developed in juveniles, reduced, but still visible, in adults. Plastron closes tightly, and has a broad anterior lobe, and a wide, deep anal notch; it has slight concavity in males. Head wide, with a pointed snout and 2 tentacles beneath the chin. Upper jaw has a shallow notch on each side. Easily identified by colour, as the black carapace contrasts strongly with the yellow bridge and plastron. There may be dark edges to the intergular and adjacent scutes; darker staining occurs on the plastron in some old individuals. Head black above and on the sides, sometimes with pale sutures to the parietals. Skin of the upper and lower jaws, tympanum region, and throat pale yellow, as is the iris of the eye. Limbs dark above, and yellow below.

Habitat Prefer swamps and water holes in streams in dense primary forest.
Distribution Currently known only from Gabon, but possibly entering adjacent Congo-Brazzaville.
Biology Only recently described (2000) and still poorly known. Shy species living in small water bodies in forest. Bask on fallen logs when undisturbed, but readily dive beneath undercut banks when danger threatens. Diet comprises aquatic insects and amphibians, particularly platannas (*Xenopus* and *Hymenochirus* spp.). Aestivate in soft soil during the dry season (July to October). May bite when handled, and readily give off a foul musk. The only breeding data for this species is of a female that laid a single egg (21 x 45 mm).

Adult Maran's Hinged Terrapin.

CONSERVATION Not known to be threatened, although they are caught in fish traps and retained for eating.

Lowland forest swamp in Luango National Park, Gabon.

Dwarf Hinged Terrapin
Pelusios nanus   Laurent 1956

Other common name: **African Dwarf Mud Turtle**
Named for its small size (Greek *nanos* = dwarf).

Description The smallest Side-necked terrapin (up to 120 mm). Carapace elongated and oval, flattened dorsally, lacks a vertebral keel, and may have a slightly flared posterior margin. Plastron large, with a long, broad anterior lobe, and a weakly developed hinge. Posterior lobe broad, with an anal notch, and is slightly constricted at the abdominal-femoral seam. Males small, with an obvious plastral concavity. Axillary and inguinal scutes absent, and the pectoral scute does not contact the bridge. Head has a short, blunt snout; upper jaw only slightly notched; 2 tentacles beneath the chin. Forelimbs lack large transverse scales. Carapace brown, often with dark streaks. Plastron yellow with a black border and black bridge.

Habitat Inhabit small water bodies in moist savannah.

Distribution This species is similar to more northerly Adanson's Hinged Terrapin, and seems to replace it in the savannahs bordering the southern edge of the Congo Basin, from Zambia to Angola.

Biology Very poorly known despite their wide distribution. Secretive and easily overlooked. In Zambia, known to have inhabited small ponds during the dry season. It is not known whether they aestivate at this time. Captive specimens may forage out of the water, indicating that they may hunt some of their food in dense waterside vegetation.

One Zambian female laid 5 fertile eggs (28–30 mm x 15–17 mm) but these did not hatch.

> **CONSERVATION** Probably not threatened, as it is small and widely distributed.

ABOVE AND LEFT: Adult Dwarf Hinged Terrapin at Mililungwe, Zimbabwe.

Black Hinged Terrapin

Pelusios niger   (Duméril and Bibron 1835)

Other common name: **Western Black Mud Turtle**

Named after the black colour of the shell
(Latin *niger* = black).

Description A very large terrapin (males to 350 mm and 4.5 kg, females to 280 mm). Oval shell elongate and domed, with a flared rear edge, serrated in juveniles, which also have a low vertebral keel. Rear edge becomes smooth, and the top of the shell flattened along the backbone, in old individuals. Vertebrals broader than they are long. Head narrow, with a protruding, pointed snout and a prominently hooked upper jaw. 3 or 4 large transverse scales on the anterior surface of the forelimbs. Plastron with a broad, short anterior lobe, and a narrow posterior lobe with a posterior notch. Plastral hinge only fully develops in juveniles with shells longer than 70 mm. Axillary and inguinal scutes absent. Shell usually black to reddish brown, sometimes with light seams, above and below. Centre of the plastron may be yellow in old individuals. Skin of the neck, chin, limbs and tail grey-yellow. Head and jaws yellow, with fine dark brown or black vermiculation. These are more conspicuous in juveniles. Carapace brown with a dark stripe running over the vertebrals in some specimens; scutes may have dark speckles and streaks, especially in juveniles. The taxonomic status of this form is being investigated.

Habitat Found in varied water bodies, including lagoons, lakes and marshes, and entering flooded savannah in the wet season. When found together with the Western Hinged Terrapin, prefer exposed seasonal swamps and marshes with little aquatic vegetation. Avoids very shallow margins and deep open water.

Distribution West Africa, from Sierra Leone and Liberia to Gabon.

Biology Aestivate underground during the dry season, when many are dug up during ploughing. Mainly carnivorous, feeding on a wide variety of small aquatic animals, but will also take water plants. Main prey, in Nigeria, small fish and tadpoles (for 70% and 30% of individuals, respectively); in Gabon, mussels and earthworms. Fallen fruit and crustaceans more frequently eaten in the dry season, and amphibian eggs and tadpoles in the wet season. Nest holes dug in grasslands with abundant vegetation and sandy soil. Clutches contain 6–18 eggs (24 x 48 mm). In Nigeria, home range size is similar for both females (3.7 ha ± 1.9 ha) and males (4.0 ha ± 1.6 ha).

ABOVE: Juvenile Black Hinged Terrapin shells.
LEFT: Adult Black Hinged Terrapin.

CONSERVATION Commonly eaten, and also exported in large numbers for the international pet trade. The colourful juveniles are in particular demand; in 2000, Togo exported over 3 000 specimens. Widely distributed, and not currently considered threatened. In coastal Nigeria, populations have been affected by oil pollution, with population declines and habitat shifts.

Thick forest vegetation crowds a river bank in Gabon.

Variable Hinged Terrapin

Pelusios rhodesianus   Hewitt 1927

Other common names: **Mashona Hinged Terrapin, Variable Mud Turtle**

Named after the country (Rhodesia , now Zimbabwe) from which the first specimens were collected.

Description A medium-sized hinged terrapin (up to 255 mm). Shell domed, elongate and smooth (a weak keel may persist towards the rear). Posterior marginals not serrated. Plastron large, covering most of the carapace opening, with a broad anterior lobe, smaller posterior lobe and a deep anal notch. Axillary absent. Head small, with a slightly projecting snout, a strongly bicuspid beak, and 2 tentacles under the chin. Front of the forelimbs with well developed, crescent-shaped scales. Carapace and plastron uniform black (in a few Zimbabwean individuals, there may be irregular yellow patches or they may even be a uniform yellow). Head brown with yellow vermiculation in northern populations, brown dorsally but yellow laterally in southern populations. Skin of the neck and limbs yellow; outer surfaces of the limbs greyish brown.

Habitat Low rivers, swamps and marshes and quiet, weed-choked backwaters on dams.

Distribution From eastern DRC and Uganda, south to Angola, entering Okavango Swamp in Botswana, central Zimbabwe and central Mozambique, with relict populations in KwaZulu-Natal.

Biology Active in the thickly vegetated backwaters and edges of shallow water. During the dry season they aestivate in among the mud and reed beds, and may be scarred when bush fires rage through the dry reed beds during the

An adult Variable Hinged Terrapin.

Lowland forest stream in the Zambezi Delta, Mozambique.

dry season. Diet largely molluscs and aquatic insects; they also feed on small fish and on the stems, leaves and flowers of aquatic plants. The female lays small clutches (11–14) of small, soft-shelled eggs (33–37 x 20–23 mm). In the Kafue Flats, Zambia, females may lay more than one clutch in a summer (nesting has been recorded September–April). The first eggs are laid immediately after the start of the summer rains. Hatchlings have been recorded in December and January, and females are sexually mature at only 139 mm long.

CONSERVATION The most southern populations in KwaZulu-Natal are under severe threat from urban encroachment and habitat loss, and are regionally threatened. Elsewhere, widespread and not known to be threatened.

Serrated Hinged Terrapin
Pelusios sinuatus   (Smith 1838)

Other common name: **East African Serrated Mud Turtle**

Named after the sinuous keel along the backbone (Latin *sinuosus* = wavy).

Description The largest hinged terrapin, with large females reaching 485 mm and weighing up to 9 kg. Shell elongated and oval, and flattened on top. Low medial keel, particularly in juveniles; vertebrals as long as they are broad or slightly longer. Posterior marginals serrated. Plastron large, only slightly smaller than the opening of the carapace, with a strong hinge. Posterior plastron lobe does not constrict, but has a large anal notch. Axillary scale at the front junction of the carapace and the plastron. Males have a slightly concave plastron. Head broad, but not overly long, with a protruding, pointed snout. Upper jaw notched and often bicuspid; 2 longish tentacles beneath the chin. Carapace and bridge uniform black, sometimes with yellowish seams. Plastron with a pale yellow centre and a sharply defined, black, angular pattern around the edge. Head blackish brown, with yellow or brown vermiculation. Skin of the neck and limbs pale olive grey.

Habitat Perennial rivers and permanent lakes and pans.

Distribution The southernmost species, extending from tropical East Africa, along the Zambezi River to Victoria Falls and south to KwaZulu-Natal, South Africa. The species previously had a wider distribution, and Lower Pleistocene fossils (3.75–1.8 Ma) are known from Chad and Lake Turkana.

Biology Common in large water bodies; usually seen basking at the surface or on logs and rocks during the day. May move to shallow pans in the wet season. During basking, head and legs fully extended to absorb heat rapidly and to dry the skin and remove parasites such as leeches. Larger specimens eat freshwater mussels; juveniles take invertebrates and frogs.

In Lake Malawi large freshwater snails form the main diet. Often scavenge at game killed by crocodiles, to which they in turn regularly fall prey. Often eat engorged ticks taken from the legs of buffalo and rhinoceros as they wallow in water holes. Juveniles may be active at night. When disturbed, retreat into their shells, and rarely bite. In captivity they have lived for over 12 years. The female lays 7–27 eggs (24–26 x 42–45 mm, 18–21 g), up to 500 m from the nearest water, between October and January. In the wild, hatchlings appear between March and April. Eggs artificially incubated (32°C) may hatch in 48 days. Hatchlings measure 40–51 mm, and weigh 12–15 g. Many nests are excavated and the eggs eaten by water monitors and mongoose.

Serrated Hinged Terrapin.

Serrated Hinged Terrapin plastron.

A backwater in the Zambezi River delta.

CONSERVATION Widespread and common; not threatened. May become a nuisance, taking baits set for fish.

Adult Serrated Hinged Terrapin.

Black-bellied Hinged Terrapin
Pelusios subniger (Lacepède 1788)

Other common names: **East African Black Mud Turtle, Pan Hinged Terrapin**

Named after its black plastron (Latin *sub* = under, *niger* = black).

Description A small terrapin (up to 200 mm in females). Shell smooth, and lacks a keel or serrated posterior margin; oval-shaped in males but more rounded in females. All vertebrals broader than they are long. Plastron with anterior lobe much broader than the posterior lobe, a small plastral hinge, an anal notch, but no axillary. Head large, with a blunt snout and smooth beak; there are usually 2 tentacles under the chin. Crescent-shaped scales on the front of the forelimbs poorly developed or absent. Males have a slight plastral concavity. Carapace uniform brown, and brown-grey when dry. Bridge yellow and brown. Plastron normally yellow with dark seams or a dark border. Head uniform brown, not vermiculated, sometimes with black spots. Jaw yellow; skin of the neck and limbs grey or black.

Subspecies Two races are recognised. The typical race, *P. s. subniger*, occurs on the African mainland and Madagascar, and is replaced on the Seychelles by *P. s. parietalis*.

Habitat Found in savannah and grassland, where they inhabit pools in seasonal rivers and streams, and pans and temporary water bodies such as swamps and marshes.

Distribution East Africa, from Burundi and Tanzania westward to eastern DRC, Zambia, and northern Botswana. In the south they enter Zimbabwe and northern Botswana, reaching the upper Limpopo River, southern Mozambique (including the Bazaruto Archipelago), and northern regions of the Kruger National Park, South Africa. Occur on Madagascar and the Seychelles, and have been introduced to Gloriosa Island (now extinct), Mauritius Island (possibly extinct), and Diego Garcia of the Chagos Archipelago.

Biology Prefer temporary, seasonal pans with aquatic vegetation. Aestivate on land during droughts, when they may be scarred by dry season fires. May wander over land between water bodies during the rainy season. May eat small frogs, aquatic invertebrates and even water plants. May discharge their cloacal contents in defence. Females probably nest throughout the wet season. Clutches number 8–12 soft-shelled elliptical eggs (36 x 21 mm). Incubation takes 104–107 days (28°C) or 58 days (30°C). Hatchlings measure 30–35 mm. Females are sexually mature at around 170 mm.

Adult Black-bellied Hinged Terrapin.

Head of adult Black-bellied Hinged Terrapin.

The Seychelles race is considered Critically Endangered, due to deterioration of its habitat. Population reduced to only 400–450 adults. Although the mainland populations are not considered threatened, the increasing incidence of man-induced fires to improve cattle grazing in the African savannah is of concern. Runaway fires can both kill aestivating terrapins during the dry season, and also burn reed beds and marsh vegetation, changing the nutrient content and productivity of pans when they fill in the wet season, and causing fast evaporation. The terrapins are then more easily caught by people, for both eating and export for the pet trade. They may be extending their range in central Zimbabwe by using man-made water bodies such as borrow pits and small farm dams.

Marshy habitat of the Black-bellied Hinged Terrapin.

Upemba Hinged Terrapin
Pelusios upembae   Broadley 1981

Named after the region Upemba in the eastern DRC, from which it was first collected.

Description A medium-sized terrapin (up to 230 mm) with an elongated, oval, flattened shell, with a smooth rear border. Plastron closes tightly and is notched posteriorly; intergular broader than it is long. Head large and broad, with a blunt snout, smooth upper jaw and 2 tentacles beneath the chin. Skin of the neck and throat finely granulated. Shell dark brown to black above, and black below, with yellow patches or blotches along the central seam. Head uniformly yellow-brown above, often with fine yellow vermiculation, yellow below.

The skin of the neck and limbs is finely granular and yellow-brown.

Habitat Deep streams and rivers in the eastern tributaries of the Congo River.

Distribution Restricted to the Fungwe and Lualaba watersheds of the DRC, including the Upemba lakes bordering the Lualaba River.

Biology Biology unknown, due to its restricted range and the political turmoil in the region, preventing further study since its description in 1981. Once confused with the Okavango Hinged Terrapin, and probably has a similar lifestyle.

RIGHT: Different views of the shell of an adult Upemba Hinged Terrapin.

> **CONSERVATION** Possibly threatened, as it has a restricted range and is known to be eaten by local people.

Upemba Hinged Terrapin habitat in the headwaters of the Congo River.

Williams' Hinged Terrapin
Pelusios williamsi   Laurent 1965

Other common name: **Williams' Mud Turtle**

Named in honour of Ernest E. Williams, Emeritus Professor of Biology at the Museum of Comparative Zoology, Harvard University.

Description A relatively large species (to 250 mm). Carapace elongate, oval and moderately depressed in the centre. Vertebral keel low, blunt and more prominent in juveniles. Posterior marginals faintly serrated in juveniles, becoming smooth in adults. Plastron large, covering most of the carapacial opening, with a medium anal notch; posterior lobe is longer than the anterior lobe. Intergular wide and, depending upon region, may be long (typical race) or short (*P.w. lutescens*). Bridge wide but lacks an axillary scute. Head broad, with a slightly protruding snout; upper jaw with a pair of tooth-like cusps; 2 tentacles beneath the chin. Front of each forelimb with a number of enlarged transverse scales. Carapace black to dark brown. Plastron mainly black with yellow seams and irregular yellow blotches, restricted mainly to the centre of the plastron (*P.w. lutescens* and *P.w. williamsi*), or mainly yellow with grey or brown spotting (*P. w. laurenti*). Head and limbs brown; limb sockets yellow.

Head of an adult Willams' Hinged Terrapin.

Lake Victoria, the largest of Africa's Great Lakes, is home to the Lake Victoria Hinged Terrapin.

Subspecies Three subspecies, best distinguished by their plastron colour, are recognised. The typical race (*Pelusios w. williamsi*, the Lake Victoria Hinged Terrapin) inhabits the upper Nile drainage around Lake Victoria. The Albert Nile Hinged Terrapin (*P. w. lutescens*) occurs in the west of the range, in the Lake Edward-Semliki-Lake Albert drainage; the Ukerewe Island Hinged Terrapin (*P. w. laurenti*) is known only from Ukerewe Island, Lake Victoria, and is also characterised by a laterally constricted first vertebral.

Habitat Lakes, rivers and swamps.

Distribution Endemic to the upper Nile basin, including lakes Victoria, Albert and Edward.

Adult Lake Victoria Hinged Terrapin.

Biology Unstudied and poorly known. Reported to prefer deep water and to be carnivorous. In captivity nests were dug about 20 cm deep in moist soil. Clutches of 7–18 elongate eggs (21 x 40 mm) were laid and hatched after 59–84 days incubation. The hatchlings weighed 8–11 g.

CONSERVATION The Lake Victoria region is subject to massive human population growth and habitat loss due to farming and fishing. In addition to human harvesting, this terrapin may be endangered by the introduction of Nile Perch as a fishery in Lake Victoria. Ukerewe, a rocky island with smaller hills, is 50 km long and between 25 and 35 km wide, and heavily populated. The island race, if taxonomically valid, is particularly threatened due to its very restricted range.

Sea Turtles

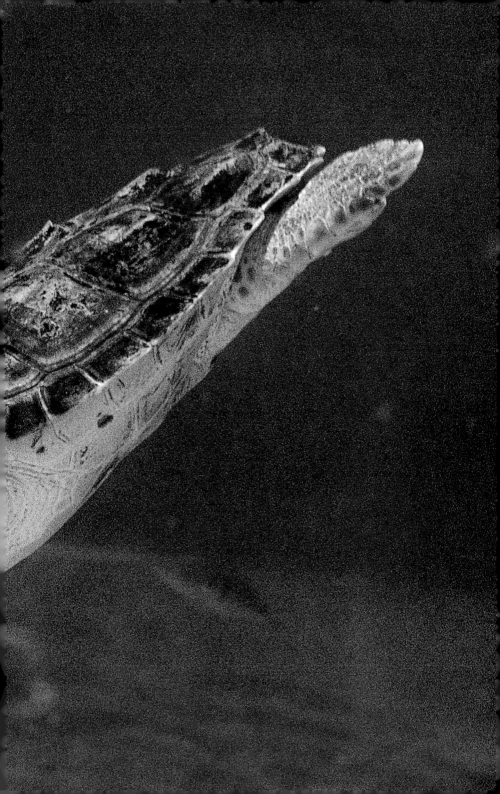

Sea Turtles

The first chelonians lived in swamps, but by the Cretaceous period at least four families had moved into the oceans. Many of these early sea turtles were large, the largest being the giant *Archelon*, which was nearly 4 m long. Modern sea turtles are less diverse, and are represented by only seven species in two families; one of these, the Leatherback Turtle, is highly aberrant. They display certain primitive features, including an inability to retract the head or limbs, a robust skull and a row of inframarginals along the bridge. Other unusual features, adaptations to marine life,

A hatchling Green Sea Turtle.

include the excretion of excess salt via the tear ducts and the modification of the limbs into flippers, which retain only 1 or 2 claws; when swimming, flippers are 'rowed' in unison rather than used alternately as are the limbs of terrapins.

All sea turtles are tied to land for reproduction, and must haul themselves ashore to lay their eggs. Clumsy and almost helpless on land, the breeding females are easy to kill. Although shy when they first emerge to nest, once they start laying eggs, they ignore all disturbance. Their numbers have been decimated and all species are now endangered. They all mate and nest in a similar fashion, crawling ashore onto sheltered, sandy beaches, often on moonless nights. They dig a deep pit and lay large numbers of spherical, soft-shelled eggs. They emerge from the water between one and 10 times at 10–15-day intervals during a breeding season, and may lay up to 1 000 eggs in a season. Females breed at 2 to 5-year intervals, but many breed only once and the interval varies between species and individuals. Hatchling sex is determined by incubation temperature; the critical period is the third week of incubation, and higher temperatures (32–34°C) produce mainly females, whilst males hatch from cooler nests.

TURTLES UNDER THREAT

All sea turtles are threatened, and their numbers have declined worldwide. All seven recognised species are listed as either Endangered or Critically Endangered in the World Conservation Union (IUCN) *Red List of Threatened Species 2007*. Traditionally, the main threat has been unsustainable harvesting; breeding females are particularly vulnerable when they come ashore to lay their eggs. More modern threats include the loss of nesting beaches due to coastal development. Beach housing has a secondary impact; bright house lights disorientate emerging hatchlings and returning females, which crawl towards the lights and away from the water. Nearly 6% of female Loggerhead Turtles at the major rookery in Pongara National Park, Gabon, mistakenly head inland after nesting, confused by light pollution. Modern fisheries, using trawl nets and longlines, also kill countless sea turtles, and between 2 000 and 5 000 turtles are killed every year in shrimp nets on the Sofala Bank, northern Mozambique. These deaths could easily be avoided by the incorporation of 'Turtle Excluder' devices in the net mouths. Marine pollution, in all its different forms, threatens all sea life, including sea turtles. To compound these existing threats, global warming will cause sea levels to rise and some nesting beaches may become inundated. As the sex of sea turtle eggs is determined by the incubation temperature, a rise of 1°C could reduce the numbers of male turtles born, and a 3°C rise could cause high levels of infant mortality.

With protection measures and public education, sea turtles can survive. The Green Sea Turtle rookery on Ascension Island, in the mid-Atlantic, has made a wonderful recovery since the nesting beaches were protected, and it has grown almost 300% in the last 30 years. Turtle populations on nesting beaches at Poilão in the Bajargos Archipelago, Guinea Bissāu, show a similar recovery. The Leatherback Turtle colony in KwaZulu-Natal recovered from a low of five nesting females in 1966 to a high of 168 in 2000, and is now stable. The Indian Ocean islands of Europa and Aldabra, both of whose turtle populations were virtually wiped out by the early 1920s, now host thousands of nesting Green Sea Turtles, and similar recoveries have been recorded on other protected islands in the region.

Modern Sea Turtles
FAMILY CHELONIIDAE

These are advanced sea turtles that retain a hard shell and have flipper-like limbs to allow more efficient swimming. The plastron and carapace are connected by ligaments rather than a bony bridge. Numerous fossils are known since the Cretaceous period, with over 33 genera, of which only five are still living. Four genera are represented in African coastal waters. Flatback sea turtles, previously placed with Green Sea Turtles, are now placed in a separate genus (*Natator depressus*). They are restricted to Australasian waters, and characterised by their flat shells, carnivorous habits, and small clutch size.

Green Sea Turtles often come ashore to bask on the Skeleton Coast of Namibia to escape the cold Benguela current.

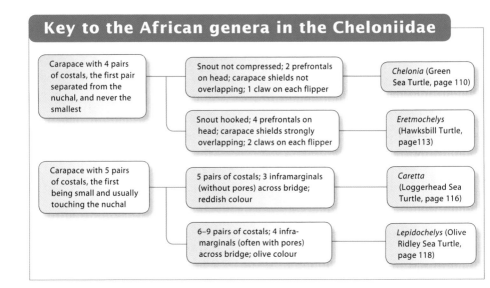

Key to the African genera in the Cheloniidae

Carapace with 4 pairs of costals, the first pair separated from the nuchal, and never the smallest	Snout not compressed; 2 prefrontals on head; carapace shields not overlapping; 1 claw on each flipper	*Chelonia* (Green Sea Turtle, page 110)
	Snout hooked; 4 prefrontals on head; carapace shields strongly overlapping; 2 claws on each flipper	*Eretmochelys* (Hawksbill Turtle, page113)
Carapace with 5 pairs of costals, the first being small and usually touching the nuchal	5 pairs of costals; 3 inframarginals (without pores) across bridge; reddish colour	*Caretta* (Loggerhead Sea Turtle, page 116)
	6–9 pairs of costals; 4 inframarginals (often with pores) across bridge; olive colour	*Lepidochelys* (Olive Ridley Sea Turtle, page 118)

Green Sea Turtle

Chelonia Brongniart 1800

Widely distributed; only one species is currently recognised. The generic name derives from the Greek (*chelone* = tortoise or turtle).

Green Sea Turtle

Chelonia mydas   (Linnaeus 1758)

Named because of its aquatic habitat (Greek *mydos* = wetness, dampness). The common name comes not from the shell colour, but from the characteristic green body fat.

Description A large, hard-shelled sea turtle (females average 98–120 cm, to 140 cm). Individuals in the Indian Ocean do not grow as large as those in the Atlantic, with the largest female nesting on the Mozambique islands weighing 208 kg. (There are old records of Atlantic Ocean Green Sea Turtles weighing up to 300 kg, but such giants no longer exist.) Shell rounded, flat and smooth, with thin, non-overlapping scutes, and a median keel in juveniles, disappearing in adults. 12 pairs of marginals, the posterior ones serrated in juveniles and smooth in adults. 4 pairs of costals. Plastron relatively large, with 2 long ridges in the young. Bridge wide, with 4 inframarginals that lack pores. Head compact and relatively small, with undivided, elongate prefrontal scales on the nose and a strong beak. Single claw on each flipper (2 on front flipper in juveniles). Males with much longer tails than females, and a greatly enlarged claw on the forelimb. Coloration varied. Carapace in hatchlings black-brown, with bronze highlights on the vertebrals, and a white border and plastron. Juvenile carapace initially dark grey but, in turtles over 20 cm long, the ground

A young adult Green Sea Turtle.

colour varies from pale red-brown to dark brown, with yellow, dark brown, or red-brown streaks. Carapace in adults varies from greenish brown to black; streaking may persist, break into spots or fade completely. Plastron dirty white to yellow. Head shields black to red-brown, and often white-edged. Females usually darker than males.

Subspecies None are currently recognised. The Black Turtle of the eastern Pacific Ocean is sometimes recognised as a valid race or even full species (*C. agassizi*), but recent genetic studies indicate that it is poorly differentiated from typical Green Sea Turtles and that it is probably best treated simply as a melanistic population.

Habitat Forages in shallow waters and estuaries with abundant seaweed; will cross deep open ocean on breeding migrations. Usually restricted to warm waters (>20°C), although they may be occasional vagrants in colder seas.

Distribution Circumtropical and subtropical seas. Found in all African coastal waters, although not feeding in the cold Benguela Current off the western Cape coast.

Biology The most omnivorous sea turtles, feeding during the first year of life on jellyfish and other floating organisms. Thereafter, predominantly herbivorous, grazing on a large variety of seaweeds (green, brown, and red algae), as well as more typical plants including mangrove (roots and leaves) and sea grasses such as *Zostera*, *Thalasila*, *Halophila* and others, in estuaries and shallow seas.

A hatchling Green Sea Turtle with white-edged shields.

Subadults and occasional adults common in coastal waters; some become temporary residents in open estuaries.

Most sea turtles bask at the surface in calm seas, but the cold waters of the Benguela Current, off Namibia's Skeleton Coast, may drive adults to bask on the shore. As their diet contains so much plant material, it is poor in vitamin D, and it has been suggested that they need to bask more than other sea turtles in order to manufacture vitamin D by the action of sunlight on skin sterols. In the Gulf of California, Green turtles overwinter on the sea bottom, but it is doubtful whether this behaviour occurs in African waters, where sea turtles probably migrate seasonally to warm waters.

Both males and females migrate to the breeding beaches. Mating takes place in shallow water close to shore, although mating pairs have been seen more than 1 km from shore.

Sea Turtles

Green Sea Turtles nesting on Europa Island, Mozambique Channel.

A nesting Green Sea Turtle.

Copulation occurs as pairs float at the surface, and may last several days. Several males (up to 5) may simultaneously court and attempt to mate with a single female. The male hooks the enlarged claws of the front flippers over the leading edge of the female's carapace, and also uses the strong nail at the tip of the prehensile tail to provide further anchorage. After mating, the females may store the sperm for use in subsequent egg clutches.

When a clutch of eggs is ready to be laid, the female comes ashore on a favoured beach and moves up the beach by 'humping', moving both forelegs together as if swimming (all other sea turtles move on land by moving alternate limbs). The eggs are spherical (41–47 mm in diameter, 38–58 g) and 115–197 are laid in each clutch. The female returns 2–3 (up to 6) times at intervals of 10–20 days. Eggs hatch in about 56 days, the young emerging together, usually at night. Carapace length in hatchlings is 45–51 mm, and they weigh 18–29 g. Sexual maturity is reached at 6–13 years in captivity, but later in the wild, possibly only at 19–24 years. Males have fully developed tails at shell lengths of around 75 cm, whilst females mature between 65 and 83 cm.

Nesting beaches Relatively few Green turtle rookeries along the Atlantic seaboard; numerous nesting sites now either extinct or drastically reduced in number. The most significant nesting site in western Africa occurs at Poilão in the Bijargos Archipelago, Guinea Bissãu ❶, where 2 000 females nest each year. Small numbers also nest on Bioko Island in the Gulf of Guinea, and also on the beaches of Gabon and around the mouth of the Congo River, including Cabinda. Nests in Namibe Province, southern Angola, December to March.

The most extensive Green turtle populations in the western Indian Ocean occur in Arabian waters, with very large nesting grounds in Oman (Ras Al Hadd, 7 000 females a year, and other beaches) and Yemen (Makulla, 10 000 females a year). Scattered nesting also occurs on the main islands, including Madagascar, Seychelles, Mauritius, with perhaps 5 000–10 000 nesting females.

The main rookery on Europa Island in the Mozambique Channel ❷, where 10 000–20 000 turtles nest annually, is the main stronghold for Green turtles in eastern Africa. A few Green turtles also nest on the archipelagos of Bazaruto, Primeiras, Segundas and Quirimbas in Mozambique, with scattered mainland nesting sites in northern Tanzania and Kenya. Maziwe Island (Pemba) was the most important rookery in East Africa, but is now underwater due to erosion. The most concentrated numbers of nests now appear to be on the small offshore islands of Zanzibar, Mafia and possibly the Songo Songo Archipelago.

Although there are numerous records of Green turtles nesting on beaches on the African mainland from Somalia to Senegal, few remain viable due to overexploitation.

Hawksbill Turtles

Eretmochelys   Fitzinger 1843

Medium-sized, highly distinctive sea turtles. Only a single species recognised. Fossils related to the living species are known from early Pliocene deposits (4.5–5 Ma) in Florida. Recent genetic analysis has shown that Hawksbill turtles are more closely related to Loggerhead and Ridley turtles than to Green and Flatback turtles.

The generic name alludes to the turtle's oar-like flippers (Greek *eretmon* = oar, and *chelys* = tortoise or turtle).

Hawksbill Sea Turtle

Eretmochelys imbricata   (Linnaeus 1766)

Named after the overlapping shell scutes
(Latin *imbricatus* = imbricate, overlapping).

Description A small sea turtle that rarely exceeds a metre in length and weighs 35–77 kg, although old giants up to 114 cm and 139 kg have been reported. Shell scales thick and overlapping. Head narrow and anteriorly pointed, with a long, slightly bird-like beak (hence its common name). 2 pairs of prefrontals, 4 pairs of costals and 12 pairs of marginals, the posterior ones markedly serrated. 4 inframarginals that lack pores. Forelimbs have very long digits, with 2 claws on each limb. Males have longer tails and narrower carapaces than females, and a small plastral concavity. Carapace in hatchlings heart-shaped with a central keel, and uniform brown in colour. Plastron, with 2 longitudinal ridges, is dark, each scale having a large, dark spot. Carapace shields, in adults, translucent amber and beautifully patterned with irregular, radiating streaks of light red-brown, black and yellow. Plastron uniform yellow to orange-yellow. Head yellowish, with black-centred scales.

Subspecies Two doubtful subspecies have been described, based on minor shell

A Hawksbill Turtle nesting on a coral reef.

Biology Omnivorous, but they prefer invertebrates, particularly sponges. Few other vertebrates can eat sponges, as many are toxic and they also contain tiny silica spines that can cause physical damage to the intestines. Although some populations, for instance that in the Caribbean, feed largely on sponges, other animals are also eaten, including jellyfish, hydroids, coral, polychaete worms, anemones, sea urchins, molluscs such as bivalves and cephalopods, tunicates, and even fish. Plants and seaweed are taken, particularly by juveniles that eat floating seaweed, such as *Sargassum*.

differences that may, however, be related to age. The typical race, *E. i. imbricata*, occurs in the Atlantic, whilst *E. i. bissa* ranges through the Indo-Pacific oceans.

Habitat Usually found among coral reefs in tropical waters, but may enter shallow coastal waters, including mangrove bays, estuaries and muddy lagoons.

Distribution Circumtropical, but absent from the Mediterranean, and found only as a rare vagrant to southern Cape coastal waters. The cold Benguela Current prevents the movement of Indian Ocean Hawksbills into Atlantic tropical waters. Hawksbills tagged in Brazil have been recovered in Corisco Bay, on the border of Equatorial Guinea and Gabon.

Eating the flesh and eggs of Hawksbills is dangerous, as they may store in their tissues toxins from various poisonous sea organisms that they eat.

Mating occurs in shallow water off the nesting beaches, although excited males may even follow a female onto the beach. Females are wary when emerging at night to breed, and come out in small groups at irregular intervals. Nesting occurs at night and takes about an hour. Females breed in 3-year cycles. The number of eggs in a clutch varies from 50 to 200 (average 130–160), depending on the region and the size of the female. The eggs are usually spherical with a diameter of 35–42 mm. Females

Luango National Park, Gabon, where four species nest, has Africa's most important sea turtle nesting beaches.

lay 2–4 clutches at 15-day to 19-day intervals during the season. After incubation (52–74 days), the hatchlings, measuring 39–50 mm, emerge at night, or sometimes in the early morning, and move quickly to the sea. Growth is relatively rapid, and sexual maturity is reached in 8–10 years (4 years in captivity).

Nesting beaches Due to their small size and the danger posed by predators, they nest mainly on isolated offshore islands, preferring beaches of coarse sand. Few mainland nesting sites known. A few nests reported on Los, Roume, Tamara and Blanche islands in Guinea, and Bioko Island in Equatorial Guinea.

The most significant nesting occurs on the islands of São Tome and Principe ❶. The most southerly records for the Atlantic occur on the beaches of Gabon (Ndindi) and Djeno and Foko in the Congo. Unconfirmed reports of nesting in Angola from Cabinda to Namibe Province.

Nesting on the east coast is rare; the main Indian Ocean rookeries are in northeast Madagascar, Tromelin Island, and Primeiras and St Brandon islands in Mauritius. Nesting along the East African coast has only been recorded in low numbers on remote offshore islands such as Misali and Mnemba in Zanzibar, the small islands off Dar es Salaam, Shungimbili Island in northwest Mafia and Songo Songo Archipelago. The most important nesting sites in Tanzania are Misali Island, off Pemba, and Mafia Island. In 2001, over 600 Hawksbill nests were discovered on the beaches of Vamizi and Rongui in the Querimba Islands, northern Mozambique ❷.

No recent reports of nesting further south. In the western Indian Ocean, Seychelles has the largest population of nesting Hawksbills (1 000–2 000 nesting females annually). Other rookeries include the Chagos Archipelago (300–700) and Sultanate of Oman (600–800).

> **CONSERVATION** Critically endangered turtle whose survival depends on active conservation. Throughout the tropical seas, wild populations are overexploited for their shell, and their meat is also eaten.

TORTOISESHELL JEWELLERY AND ORNAMENTS

The scutes of Hawksbill turtles are used to make 'tortoiseshell' (*bekko*) jewellery and ornaments. Their use in Japan dates back to the Genroku Period (1688–1704), and forms a key part of the traditional Japanese wedding dress. Translucent tortoiseshell is a beautiful clear amber, streaked with red, white, green, brown and black. Before the scutes are removed by the application of heat, the turtle is usually killed. There is evidence that, if the scutes are removed carefully and the turtle is returned to the sea, it can regenerate lost scutes. A single turtle usually yields only 780 g of tortoiseshell (called *carey* in the Caribbean).

The volume of global trade is horrendous. In 1978–9, Indonesia and Japan imported 260 000 kg of raw shell; over 600 000 turtles were killed between 1970 and 1986 to supply the *bekko* imported into Japan. In Singapore and the Phillipines, the dried, polished bodies of nearly 100 000 juveniles are sold as curios annually. Most tortoiseshell ornaments are now made in Vietnam and Indonesia. Trade statistics indicate that there have been massive declines – up to 95% – in Hawksbill populations in countries such as Madagascar and the Seychelles.

Antique hair combs made of tortoiseshell.

Save this critically endangered species – don't buy tortoiseshell.

Loggerhead Sea Turtles

Caretta   Rafinesque 1814

This genus contains a single living species, and a number of indeterminate fossil forms dating back to the late Cretaceous period of Europe.

The generic name is descriptive (Latin version of the French *caret* = turtle, tortoise or sea turtle).

Loggerhead Sea Turtle

Caretta caretta   (Linnaeus 1758)

Named by duplicating the genus name.

Description A very large turtle, usually attaining a size of nearly a metre, and weighing about 100–150 kg. The largest living hard-shelled turtle, surpassed in size only by the Leatherback turtles. Although historical weights of up to 450 kg have been claimed, these are very doubtful. Few, if any, Loggerheads reach even 200 kg. Shell elongate, tapering at the rear; smooth in adults, but has median keels on the costals and vertebrals in juveniles. 5 pairs of costals and 11–12 pairs of marginals, bluntly serrated at the rear in juveniles. Plastron has 3 inframarginals without pores, and 2 long keels in hatchlings. Head very broad, with 2 pairs of prefrontals and strong jaws with extensive crushing surfaces. Each limb has 2 claws. Males have more massive heads and longer tails than females, and an enlarged, strongly curved claw on each front flipper. In hatchlings, the carapace, plastron and head a uniform brown of varying shades; skin of the neck and flippers darker. In both juveniles and adults, the carapace and the top of the head are uniform red-brown, with white-edged scales. Plastron uniform yellowish; skin light yellowish grey.

Subspecies Two poorly defined subspecies have been proposed, with the typical race, *C. c. caretta*, being restricted to the Atlantic, and the other, *C. c. gigas*, to the Indo-Pacific. This is very doubtful and recent genetic studies reveal low divergence between the populations and do not support recognition of subspecies.

Habitat Migrate across open seas, and has been found 240 km from land, but feed in coastal waters and reefs and enter bays, lagoons, salt marshes, creeks and the mouths of large rivers.

Distribution Found worldwide in temperate and subtropical waters. More common on the east than on the west coast of Africa.

An adult Loggerhead Turtle at Aliwal Reef, South Africa.

Biology Drift in surface waters for at least the first 3 years of life, eating mainly bluebottles and comb jellies. Subsequently, search for food in shallow coastal waters, becoming increasingly carnivorous. The extremely strong jaws are well adapted for crushing hard-bodied food, and they feed on almost all reef invertebrates, including sponges, hydroids, jellyfish, polychaete worms, cephalopods (squid, cuttlefish), snails, whelks, conchs, bivalves (clams, mussels, oysters, scallops), barnacles and crabs. If they can catch them they also eat fish and even young turtles. Can become semidormant in cold waters, staying submerged for up to 7 hours at a time and surfacing for only 7 minutes to recover. Maturity occurs at carapace lengths of 60–70 cm, which may take 10–30 years in the wild (16–17 years in captivity). Most Loggerheads that reach adulthood live for longer than 30 years, and may live past 50 years.

A female Loggerhead nests on a beach at Maputaland.

Long migrations are often made between the feeding areas and the nesting beaches. Mating may start several months before the turtles arrive at the nesting beach, but continues throughout the period, during the day and night. The courting male circles the female, during which he may bite her neck and shoulder. Females display either passive acceptance or violent resistance. Mating occurs at the surface of the water and the female is usually completely submerged. Paired Loggerheads may copulate for up to 3 hours. Females can store sperm for some time, and multiple males may contribute sperm to a single clutch of eggs.

Nesting occurs on temperate zone beaches, and nests are usually excavated above the high tide mark at the base of the dune front. Nests are normally dug at night (occasionally during the day), and during periods of high tides. A body pit is first dug, within which a flask-shaped nest cavity about 15–25 cm deep and 20–25 cm wide is excavated with the hind limbs. During a breeding season a female lays about 500 eggs (40–42 mm in diameter) in batches of about 120 (23–198) at about 11–15-day intervals (varying from 9–28 days). Most return to nest after 2–3 years, but some may exceptionally

An exhausted female returns to the sea after laying.

take up to 8 years before breeding again, and others breed more frequently (up to 6 times in 9 years). Incubation of the eggs takes 47–66 days; hatchlings measure 39–49 mm, and usually emerge at night.

Nesting beaches Few confirmed nesting sites along the Atlantic coast, except for the Cape Verde Archipelago. Nesting sites in the Canary islands now extinct. In the Cape Verdes, over 3 000 nesting females use the beaches of Sal, Boa Vista and São Vicente, making it the largest rookery in the eastern Atlantic. Nesting in northern Angola has recently been confirmed, with 210 nests recorded in 2005 on the beach at Rio Longa, some 200 km south of Luanda ❶.

The nesting beach at Maputaland in northern KwaZulu-Natal, South Africa.

Nesting in the subtropical waters of the east coast includes the sandy beaches of Maputaland in KwaZulu-Natal ❷, and adjacent Mozambique, where 400–500 females breed each year (laying more than 2 000 eggs). A few Loggerheads also nest on the archipelagos of Bazaruto, Primeiras, Segundas and Quirimbas in Mozambique. The largest known nesting populations of Loggerheads are those on Masirah Island (Oman), where a minimum of 30 000 females nest annually.

CONSERVATION Endangered; many nesting sites are badly affected by overexploitation or from residential and recreational areas on beaches and coastal islands. Many adults are also drowned when caught in shrimp trawls or on longlines.

Ridley Sea Turtles

Lepidochelys Fitzinger 1843

The smallest of the sea turtles, with unusually broad shells.
Once famed for breeding in *arribadas*, when up to 46 000 turtles emerged to breed on a few kilometres of beach in a single day. Although this resulted in a tremendous wastage of turtle eggs, as females often dug up the eggs laid only minutes earlier by other females, it served to swamp predators, resulting in the survival of most of the hatchlings. (Sadly, man is a very efficient predator: many thousands of breeding females were butchered and sold as food in city markets.) They are the only sea turtles known to lay their eggs during the day. Only two species are recognised, and both occur in African waters, although one (Kemp's Ridley) is mainly restricted to the western Atlantic, occurring sporadically in the eastern Atlantic.
The generic name alludes to the great number of scutes (for instance, 6–9 pairs of costals) on the shell of the turtle (Greek *lepido* = scale, and *chelys* = tortoise or turtle). The origin of the name 'Ridley' is unknown.

Olive Ridley Sea Turtle

Lepidochelys olivacea (Eschscholtz 1829)

Named after the olive colour of the shell.

Description A very small sea turtle (to 73 cm, weighing 45 kg). Shell heart-shaped, smooth and flat-topped, with 5 vertebrals and numerous costal shields (5–9 on each side). Hatchlings and juveniles have 3 dorsal keels, and 2 on the plastron. 2–14 marginals, which are slightly serrated at the rear. 4 inframarginals, each with a pore on its posterior edge. Head wide, with a short, broad snout and 2 pairs of prefrontals. Each limb with 2 claws. Males have longer tails than females, and narrower, strongly tapered shells, with more intense pigmentation, and a strongly developed, curved claw on each front flipper. Hatchling carapace uniform grey-black, with light areas on the plastron, becoming more extensive in a few months; adult carapace dark to light olive green dorsally, with a pale yellow, almost white plastron.

Subspecies None are recognised; the Caribbean turtle, *L. kempii*, is now treated as a separate species.

Habitat Shallow, coastal waters and major estuaries, including shallow water between reefs and shore, larger bays and lagoons.

Distribution Circumglobal, usually in tropical waters of the Atlantic, Indian and Pacific oceans. In the eastern Pacific, the Olive Ridely Sea Turtle is found from the Galápagos, north to California, even reaching the Gulf of Alaska during El Niño years.

Biology A common sea turtle that feeds, sometimes at considerable depths, on bottom-living crustaceans, particularly prawns and shrimps, but also crabs, fish, squid, snails, oysters, sea urchins and jellyfish. Seaweeds are occasionally eaten, and small turtles even eat dead insects floating on the surface. Sometimes form large aggregations, migrating between nesting beaches and feeding grounds.

Many sleep floating at the surface, unlike other sea turtles, which usually sleep on the sea floor. They are relatively precocious: sexual maturity is reached at 7–9 years. Most nesting females are over 60 cm long, although females as small as 55 cm may breed.

Most mating occurs offshore from the nesting beaches, but some mating also occurs in the open ocean at other times of the year. During mating, the male holds his place on the female's carapace with his forelimb claws, and possibly his tail. Females start to emerge

The track of a nesting Olive Ridley Turtle, Gamba, Gabon.

A female Olive Ridley Sea Turtle on the beach at Gamba, Gabon.

The head of an Olive Ridley Sea Turtle.

(up to 30–55 cm), and may be 17–30 cm wide. Females lay 1–3 clutches of about 100 eggs (30–168) in a season. The eggs are 32–45 mm in diameter. The incubation period is short, usually 42–62 days (up to 70 days if conditions are unfavourable).

Nesting beaches Along the Atlantic coast sporadic nesting is recorded from Senegal to the DRC. The most northerly nesting beaches are in Orango National Park, Guinea Bissau ❶. Small colonies are known to breed on beaches from the Ivory Coast to Angola, with the main rookeries in Ghana (Ningo-Prampram, Ada-Foah and Keta-Anolga), Gabon (south of Banio Lagoon, ❷) and Angola (Palmeirinhas, ❸).

Few nesting sites along the east coast, although a stray female once nested on Warner Beach in KwaZulu-Natal. Between 500 and 1 000 nests were once laid each year on the islands off northern Mozambique (Primeiras, Segundas, Quirimbas archipelagos), but the current status of nesting in the region is poorly known.

Elsewhere in the western Indian Ocean, they are known to nest in Oman. The 3 nesting beaches in Orissa on the east coast of India (Gahirmatha, Devi River mouth and Rushikulya) are the most important breeding areas. Over a period of 5–7 days, more than 100 000 turtles nest in giant *arribadas* at Gahirmatha, and tens of thousands more nest at the other sites.

from the sea to nest with a rising tide in late afternoon, often during periods of strong winds. The complete nesting, from emergence to re-entering the sea, usually takes less than one hour to complete. The female tamps down the sand over the eggs with the thickened edge of her plastron. The average duration between successive nestings is about 15–17 days, but females may retain eggs for over 60 days when weather is unfavourable for nesting.

Some females nest annually, but most females breed on a 2-year cycle. The flask-shaped nests are usually 38–42 cm deep

CONSERVATION Endangered, mainly due to the overexploitation of nesting females and their eggs. Also caught in large numbers as a by-catch in shrimp nets. The incorporation of 'Turtle Excluder' devices in shrimp nests in the Indian Ocean region would significantly reduce this loss.

Leatherback Sea Turtles

FAMILY DERMOCHELYIDAE

These large to giant sea turtles are characterised by various skull features including the lack of nasal bones, extreme reduction of the bones of the carapace and plastron, and a unique internal shell that is composed of small, polygonal bones. Four fossil genera are known, dating back to the Eocene (45 Ma).

Dermochelys Blainville 1816

Only a single living genus, *Dermochelys*, survives. The name is a combination of two Greek words (*derma* = skin or hide, and *chelys* = tortoise or turtle).

Leatherback Sea Turtle

Dermochelys coricaea   (Vandellius 1761)

Other common name: **Luth**

Named because of its leathery shell (Latin *corium* = leather, *-acea* = having the nature or colour of).

Description The largest living sea turtle (adults average 1.5–1.7 m in length). One giant Leatherback had a shell length of 291 cm, weighed 916 kg, and was found entangled in a buoy rope in Harlech harbour in Wales.

Shell deep, narrow, barrel-shaped, lacks horny scutes, and tapers to a supracaudal point above the tail. Covered with thick, smooth skin that resembles vulcanised rubber. Most internal shell bones absent, replaced by a mosaic of

A massive female Leatherback Turtle hauls herself ashore to nest in Maputaland, northern KwaZulu-Natal.

The beach at Gamba, Gabon, is the largest Leatherback nesting beach in the world.

Newfoundland, and into the Benguela Current off the Cape of Good Hope. Leatherbacks tagged in Gabon have been found on the west coast of South Africa and also in South American waters off Argentina and Brazil.

Biology One of the most unusual reptiles in the world, with numerous and sophisticated adaptations to their unique lifestyle. Highly carnivorous, particularly on invertebrates, although their diet also includes some algae and even vertebrates. Feed predominantly on jellyfish (particularly Scyphomedusae), but sea urchins, octopi, squid, molluscs, amphipods, crabs, tunicates, small fish, and even a hatchling Ridley Turtle have been eaten. The jaw has a sharp rim and the throat is packed with numerous backward-facing spines.

Leatherbacks migrate into extreme northern latitudes in search of jellyfish, which occur in high concentrations where warm and cold ocean currents mix, causing upwellings and nutrient blooms. They have been recorded in the Gulf of St. Lawrence, Canada, diving daily into water of 2.5°C; sometimes into near freezing water of 0.4°C! Because of their large size, which imparts thermal inertia, and their thick insulating fat layers, they can maintain a deep body temperature up to 18°C above that of the surrounding water. Body heat is further conserved by a countercurrent circulatory system in all the limbs. The average feeding dive reaches a depth of 60–100 m, and lasts 6–10 minutes. The returning turtle spends only 3–5 minutes at the surface before diving again. Leatherbacks have to eat prodigious numbers of jellyfish – which are 95% water, with an extremely low fat and energy content – consuming up to 50% of their own body mass a day; they may feed continuously, diving day and night. To avoid having large amounts of very cold food in their stomachs, turtles may bring large jellyfish to the surface to warm before eating them. The spines in their throat may also function like whale baleen, straining jellyfish tissue as cold water is regurgitated.

In warmer waters, where jellyfish descend to deep waters during the day, turtles feed mainly at night to avoid deeper dives.

small bony plates embedded in the skin. The largest of these are raised to form 7 prominent longitudinal keels on the back and sides, with another 5 on the plastron.

Hatchling shell covered with a mosaic of small, bead-like scales and tail dorsally keeled, both features disappearing with age. Flippers long and lack claws, although these may be present for a short time in some hatchlings. Neck short and thick. Beak bicuspid, sharp-edged and hooked. Male shell slightly flatter, more tapering at the rear, with a concave plastron. Tail in males longer than hind limbs, and almost twice the length of the female tail. In adults, carapace, flippers, head and neck black, usually with scattered white to pink spots. Plastron and lower surfaces of the head and flippers are white, suffused with pink and grey-black. Juvenile carapace and flippers blue-grey when dry and blackish when wet, with white ridges on the shell and trailing edges of flippers.

Subspecies Indo-Pacific Leatherbacks are sometimes referred to as a separate race, *D. c. schlegeli*, but this is questionable.

Habitat The only pelagic sea turtle, swimming and feeding in temperate and tropical oceans. May occasionally enter shallow waters in bays and estuaries.

Distribution Found worldwide, even migrating into the cold waters off Alaska and

Although most dives are relatively short and shallow, Leatherbacks can stay underwater for over an hour, and have reached depths of over 1 230 m: in order to survive the immense pressures experienced at these depths, leatherbacks have lost their hard shells.

Atlantic leatherbacks in Gabon may nest from November–March, and in South Africa, from October–February. Typical nesting beaches have a slope of 8–12°, and are free from coral or rock. Leatherbacks usually emerge singly, generally after 21h00 on suitable high tides. The female first scrapes a body pit and then excavates the egg chamber, 47 x 30 cm wide and 61–103 cm below the surface. Breeding occurs every 2–3 years, and during a nesting season the female lays individual clutches of about 100 eggs (50–166). Up to as many as 11 clutches (usually 5–7) are laid at intervals of 8–12 days. The eggs are spherical (49–65 mm in diameter) and incubation usually takes 60–65 (sometimes 50–78) days. Hatchlings (51–68 mm) emerge at night to avoid heavy predation by ghost crabs, sea gulls and fish. Growth is very rapid; the carapace increases in length by about 1 cm per week, and weight increases a hundredfold in 29 weeks. Sexual maturity may be reached in only 5 years, at approximately 1 400 mm carapace length.

Nesting beaches On the Atlantic seaboard the most northern nesting beaches, used sporadically, occur on the Pointe de Sangomar and Ndoss in Senegal. Occasional nesting has been recorded in the Bijagos Archipelago, Guinea, and Sherbro Island, Sierra Leone. There are scattered records for the beaches from southeast Liberia to Nigeria, with sporadic low levels of nesting on the Ivory Coast and Ghana (200–300 nests per annum), but turtles nesting there are threatened by poor protection. Regular nesting occurs on Bioko Island (❶, nearly 4 000 nests per annum) and the southern beaches of Equatorial Guinea, and also the islands of São Tome and Principe ❷.

In 2000, a major rookery was discovered on the southern beaches of Gabon ❸. From 6 000–7 000 females nest each year on a 90 km beach.

Globally, this is one of the most important nesting sites for the species.

Additional nesting beaches have been found in the DRC, Cabinda and Angola (Palmeirinhas, ❹). Minor nesting in the western Indo-Pacific region has been recorded from Kenya, Tanzania, Mozambique and the Seychelles.

The most southerly nesting beach is the small rookery in Maputaland, South Africa ❺. In recent years, a few females have nested as far south as the Storms River mouth in the Western Cape.

CONSERVATION Endangered, due to massive declines in populations during the last 30 years. In 1996 it was estimated that the world's total population of female Leatherbacks was between 26 200 and 42 900, less than a third of that in 1980. The populations in the Atlantic have remained relatively stable, whilst those in the Indo-Pacific continue to decline dramatically, due to overexploitation of the eggs and breeding females, and loss to fisheries as by-catch. Many Asian and Pacific populations are on the brink of extinction. At Terengganu, Malaysia, only 20 nests a year are now found, compared with 10 000 nests a year in the 1950s. Some Leatherbacks have died after ingesting large sheets of clear plastic litter that float in the sea and are mistaken for jellyfish.

A hatchling Leatherback crawls to an uncertain future.

Resources

Websites

www.chelonian.org Host site of Chelonian Research Foundation, a non-profit organisation founded in 1992 for the production, publication and support of turtle and tortoise research worldwide.

www.homopus.org A private website for the Homopus Research Foundation, dedicated to research and captive care of Padloper tortoises.

www.pelusios.com A private website dedicated to African Hinged terrapins.

www.seaturtle.org Host site of Sea Turtle Restoration Project, with good links to sea turtle threats, conservation and science, including the Marine Turtle Newsletter.

www.saherps.net Host site for the South African Reptile Conservation Assessment, the reptile Virtual Museum, and with links to the Herpetological Association of Africa.

www.tortoisetrust.org Host site of the Tortoise Trust, the world's largest tortoise and turtle organisation.

Books

Bonin, F., Devaux, B. & Dupré, A. 1996. *Toutes les Tortues du Monde.* Delachaux et Niestlé, Lausanne.

Boycott, R.C. & Bourquin, O. 2000. *The Southern African Tortoise Book. A Guide to Southern African Tortoises, Terrapins and Turtles*, revised edition. Privately published, Hilton.

Branch, W.R. 1998. *Field Guide to the Snakes and Other Reptiles of Southern Africa.* Rev. ed. Struik Publishers, Cape Town.

Ernst, C.H. & Barbour, R.W. 1989. *Turtles of the World.* Smithsonian Institution Press, Washington, D.C. & London.

Iverson, J.B. 1992. *A Revised Checklist with Distribution Maps of the Turtles of the World.* Privately published, Earlham College, Richmond, Indiana.

Serrated Hinged Terrapin.

Glossary

abdominal pertaining to the region of the abdomen; a scute on the plastron of a chelonian shell (*see* illustration, page 14).

aestivate dig underground in dry periods and lie dormant.

anal pertaining to the region of the anus; a scute on the plastron of a chelonian shell (*see* illustration, page 14).

anapsid descriptive of a skull in which there are no openings in the temporal region.

annulus (pl. annuli) a ring on the scute of a chelonian shell, representing a period of growth.

aquatic living in water.

arribada a simultaneous, mass emergence of sea turtles on to a small beach to lay their eggs. Characteristic of Ridley Sea Turtles.

areola (pl. areolae) the central region of a chelonian scute, which may be raised or hollow.

axillary pertaining to the region of the armpit; a scute on the plastron of a chelonian shell (*see* illustration, page 14).

bicuspid *see* cuspid.

bridge the part of a chelonian shell where the carapace joins the plastron.

bursa a small pocket.

buttock tubercle the enlarged, conical scale found on the rear upper part of the hind leg of some tortoises.

carapace the upper section of a chelonian shell.

chelonian a shield reptile (tortoises, turtles and terrapins).

class the taxonomic category ranking below 'phylum' and above 'order'.

cloaca the common chamber into which the urinary, digestive and reproductive systems discharge their contents, and which opens to the exterior.

clutch collective noun for all the eggs laid by a single female at one time.

condyle the knob on the back of the skull.

conical descriptive of a raised scale that narrows to a pointed centre.

costal a scute on the carapace of a chelonian shell (*see* illustration, page 14).

cranial pertaining to the skull (cranial crests are found on top of the head).

cuspid having tooth-like projections (biscuspid: having two cusps; tricuspid: having three cusps).

diapause period during which embryonic development slows.

family the taxonomic category ranking below 'order' and above 'genus'.

femoral pertaining to the upper part of the hind limb (the thigh); a scute on the plastron of a chelonian shell (*see* illustration, page 14).

genus (pl. genera) the taxonomic category ranking below 'family' and above 'species'.

girdles the supporting structure of the limbs, e.g. the hips and shoulders.

gular pertaining to the throat region; a plate on the plastron of a chelonian shell (*see* illustration, page 14).

herbivorous eating plant matter

hinge a flexible joint in the shell of some chelonians that allows the front or rear of the shell to close.

humeral pertaining to the upper part of the forelimb; a scute on the plastron of a chelonian shell (*see* illustration, page 14).

hypoplastral a bone in the plastron of a chelonian (*see* illustration, page 14).

imbricate descriptive of an overlapping scale.

infra-marginal a scute on the plastron of a sea turtle shell (*see* illustration, page 14).

intergular a scute on the plastron of a terrapin shell (*see* illustration, page 14).

invaginate to turn inside out, like a discarded sock.

keel a prominent ridge, occurring on the back of some chelonians.

lamella (pl. lamellae) any thin, plate-like or scale-like structure.

marginal a plate on the edge of the carapace of a chelonian shell (*see* illustration, page 14).

mesoplastral a bone in the plastron of a chelonian; *see* illustration, page 14.

nuchal a scute at the front of the carapace of a chelonian shell (*see* illustration, page 14).

occipital pertaining to the backbone.

The Angulate Tortoise is endemic to southern Africa.

orbit the eye socket.

order the taxonomic category ranking below 'class' and above 'family'.

oviparous reproduction by eggs which hatch outside the female's body.

parietal pertaining to the region on the crown of the head; paired bone forming part of the roof and sides of the skull; scale on the head of a reptile.

pectoral pertaining to the region of the body where the forelimbs originate; a scute on the plastron of a chelonian shell (*see* illustration, page 14).

plastron (adj. plastral) the lower surface of the chelonian shell.

pterygoid a bone in the skull of a chelonian.

quadrate a bone in the skull of a chelonian.

race a population of a species which is distinguishable from the rest of that species; a subspecies.

retractile a part that may be drawn inwards.

scale a thin, flattened, plate-like structure that forms part of the surface covering of various vertebrates, especially fishes and reptiles.

scute any enlarged scale on a reptile; the horny plates of a chelonian shell.

submarginal pertaining to the area near the margin.

subspecies see race.

supracaudal a scute at the rear of the carapace of a chelonian shell (*see* illustration, page 14).

sutures the junction of two parts which are immovably connected.

sympatric living in the same region.

taxonomy the science of classification; the arrangement of animals and plants into groups based on their natural relationships.

tricuspid *see* cuspid.

tubercle a small, rounded protuberance.

unicuspid having one cusp. *See* cuspid.

vermiculation an irregular pattern formed from a network of fine lines.

vertebral pertaining to the region of the backbone; a scute on the carapace of a chelonian shell (*see* illustration, page 14).

vestigial being smaller and of a more simple structure (a remnant) than in an evolutionary ancestor.

zonary descriptive of the concentric zones of pigment found on a scute of a chelonian shell.

Index of common names

Page numbers in **bold** represent the main species entries. Page numbers in *italics* indicate photographs.

Index of scientific names